Phonics for Reading
A Resource Book for Teachers

Gillian Brown
Professor of English as an International Language,
Research Centre for English and Applied Linguistics,
University of Cambridge

and

Kate Ruttle

General Editors

Richard Brown
and Kate Ruttle

Consultant Editor

Jean Glasberg

CAMBRIDGE UNIVERSITY PRESS

PUBLISHED BY THE PRESS SYNDICATE OF THE UNIVERSITY OF CAMBRIDGE
The Pitt Building, Trumpington Street, Cambridge CB2 1RP, United Kingdom

CAMBRIDGE UNIVERSITY PRESS
The Edinburgh Building, Cambridge CB2 2RU, United Kingdom
40 West 20th Street, New York, NY 10011-4211, USA
10 Stamford Road, Oakleigh, Melbourne 3166, Australia

Phonics for Reading
Text © Gillian Brown and Kate Ruttle 1997
Illustrations © Cambridge University Press 1997

First published 1997

Printed in the United Kingdom at the University Press, Cambridge

A catalogue record for this book is available from the British Library

ISBN 0 521 55966 9

Illustrations by Janet Simmonett

Notice to teachers
The photocopy masters in this publication may be photocopied free of charge for classroom use within the school or institution which purchases the publication. Worksheets and photocopies of them remain in the copyright of Cambridge University Press and such photocopies may not be distributed or used in any way outside the purchasing institution. Written permission is necessary if you wish to store the material electronically.

Contents

PART ONE: Introduction

What is *Phonics for Reading*?   6

    The aims of this book   7
    Sounding out spelling patterns   7

How to use this book   8

When to use this book   8

Spelling and pronunciation   10

    Fixed letter patterns   10
    Short vowels and long vowels   10
    Stressed and unstressed syllables   10
    'Grammatical words'   11

English spelling – some background   12

Accents   13

    Initial *h-*   13
    Accent variation and the teaching of phonics   13

Glossary   14

PART TWO: Teacher's pages and worksheets

(See next page for list of titles)

PART TWO: Teacher's pages and worksheets

1. Assessment
2. Counting syllables
3. Short and long vowels
4. Initial fixed letter patterns with one silent consonant
5. Hard and soft *c*
6. Fixed letter patterns at the end of words (1)
7. Fixed letter patterns at the end of words (2)
8. Magic *-e*
9. Fixed letter patterns *ee* and *ea*
10. Short vowel pronunciation of *wa-* (1)
11. Long vowel pronunciation of *wa-* (2)
12. Vowel + *ll*
13. The fixed letter pattern *-ight*
14. Stressed and unstressed syllables
15. Words ending in consonant + *le*
16. Vowel + *r* in monosyllables
17. Vowel + *re* in monosyllables
18. Vowel + *rr* in words with two syllables
19. Vowel + *w*
20. The letter *-y* in monosyllables
21. Verb forms with *-ing* (1)
22. Verb forms with *-ing* (2)
23. Plural forms
24. Verb forms with *-ed* (1)
25. Verb forms with *-ed* (2)
26. Stressed and unstressed syllables in words ending in *-y*
27. The suffixes *-y* and *-ly* for adjectives and adverbs
28. Unstressed *-er* (*-ar*, *-or*, *-re*) as a final syllable
29. Common prefixes (*a-*, *be-*, *re-*, *un-*)
30. Compound words (1) – grammatical words
31. Compound words (2) – nouns
32. Contractions

PART ONE:
Introduction

What is *Phonics for Reading*?

This book is about one aspect of the reading skill – the relationship between spelling patterns and the pronunciation of words.

As children begin to learn to read, they meet some words again and again, and gradually learn to identify them by their overall visual profile. This method allows them, after a few weeks or months, to be able to recognise a hundred or so familiar words in their written form. By the time they are seven, children probably know at least seven thousand words in their *spoken* form. If they meet one of these words in its written form, they probably won't recognise it without some help. This book aims to help children to recognise spelling patterns, to sound out the parts of the word and, by this means, to pronounce the complete word. Once they hear the word pronounced, there is a good chance that they will be able to recognise it.

Although we keep on referring to spelling in this book, it should be clear that this book is not about teaching children to spell (a difficult task in its own right). Our focus is on helping children to recognise the written form of words.

The spelling patterns in this book are those which occur frequently in the books in the Towards Independence phase of **Cambridge Reading**. A computer corpus of all the story books was constructed and the most common patterns were extracted. The list of words which appear most often in a corpus of stories for young children is, not surprisingly, different in some respects from a list produced from writing intended for adult readers. Many common grammatical words appear quite high on both lists: *the, and, to, a, I, it, was, of,* etc. (which are the first eight words, in order of frequency, in our corpus). However, personal pronouns such as *I, she, he, we, me, him, theirs* make a relatively stronger showing in children's books. Similarly, there are a great number of contracted forms (*I'm, he'll, let's, don't, can't,* etc.) as well as many instances of proper names, which are characteristic of the genre of stories for young children. And the ninth most frequent word in our corpus, *said*, like the contracted forms, occurs so often because the corpus is based on texts containing a great deal of conversation.

In this book, we show the most common spelling–sound regularities in the corpus as a whole. We concentrate on consonants, at the beginning and end of words, and we only look at common, and fairly regular, vowel patterns. The reason we concentrate on consonants is because consonants have far more stable spelling–sound relationships than vowels. Most consonant letters can be pronounced in only one or two different ways, whereas all vowel letters can, in different contexts, be pronounced in many different ways.

In writing, the ascenders and descenders of consonant letters help to construct the overall familiar visual profile of a word. As an adult reader, you can, with only a little difficulty, read a sentence with all the vowels left out, but it's quite impossible even to begin to read a sentence with the consonants left out. Compare these versions of the same sentence:

L–ttl– R–d R–d–ng H—d w–nd–r–d –nt– th– f–r–st.

–i– – –e –e– –i–i– – –oo– –a– –e–e– i– –o – –e –o–e– –.

Just as the written consonants are crucial and generally reliable visual cues, the consonant *sounds* are equally important in the pronunciation of a word.

In this book, the early worksheets and associated teacher's notes concentrate on monosyllabic words with simple short vowels (like *back, bit, shop*). We gradually introduce more complexity, with regular rules like the rule of 'magic -*e*'. (We refer to it by this traditional name which makes it clear that the -*e* provides a helpful cue to the pronunciation of the preceding vowel. It is sometimes called 'silent *e*', but is quite unlike true silent letters such as *k*- in *knight* or -*h*- in *ghost*, which do not indicate in any way how the word should be pronounced.) Words of two syllables are covered next as we look at common suffixes like -*ing* (in *flying, coming* and *dropping*), common prefixes, compound words and word stress. Finally, we consider what is indicated by the apostrophe in contracted forms (which occur as 1 word in 40 in our corpus).

Obviously, children will meet words which contain spelling patterns which we haven't dealt with. No short book like this could offer comprehensive cover of all the patterns. What we offer here is a way of approaching the phonic aspect of reading. Teachers could use this approach as a model for dealing with spelling patterns which we don't cover here.

The aims of this book

This book has three major aims:

- To help children to learn to identify some common fixed letter patterns (sometimes known as 'letter strings'). The more fixed letter patterns children know, the more they can work by analogy to 'chunk' unrecognised written words (i.e. break words up into their component letter patterns, rather than treat them as unstructured sequences of letters). For example, if children already know the words *catch* and *match* and can identify *-atch* as a rhyming pattern, they are unlikely to have much difficulty with *patch*.

- To teach children the importance of listening to the words that they sound out so that they can make sure that they are real words and that they make good sense in the context.
- To help children to learn to identify 'base words' when they appear in different forms:
  a) with different endings (*rob* → *robbed*, *torch* → *torches*)
  b) in contracted forms (*let's* = *let* + *us*, *could've* = *could* + *have*)
  c) in compounds (*birth* + *day*, *class* + *room*, *some* + *where*).

Sounding out spelling patterns

Note: In this book, spelling patterns are printed in italics (e.g. *head*). Slant brackets are used to indicate the pronunciation of a word (e.g. /hed/).

A small number of phonemic symbols are also used:
/iː/ as in *tea*, *me*
/e/ as in *hen*, *meant*
/ei/ as in *may*, *cake*
/a/ as in *mat*
/aː/ as in *palm*, *aunt* (in southern English)
/u/ as in *put*, *took*
/ə/ as in *the*, *about*, *banana* (the unstressed vowel called 'shwa')
/k/ as in *king*, *come*, *queen*

Some children come to school having already learned the names of letters. So they call *m* /em/, *a* /ei/, and *n* /en/. Obviously /em-ei-en/ doesn't sound like /man/. It seems sensible, in these cases, to build on what the child does know, the names of the letters, and to relate the names of the letters to the sounds which are usually associated with the letter. So the child should learn that the letter with the name /em/ makes the sound /m/, and the letter with the name /ei/ makes the sound /a/, and so on. Then the children can observe that the sounds /m/, /a/ and /n/ joined together make the word /man/.

It is important for children to get used to fluent sounding out. When a word begins with two consonants, those consonants should be sounded out *together*, not sounded separately followed by the little unstressed vowel /ə/. So, for the word *black*, it's important not to pronounce /bə/ followed by /lə/, since /bə – lə/ doesn't sound like the beginning of /blak/. The lips should simply be laid together for the /b/ and not parted until the tongue is already in position to pronounce the /l/. Then /bl/ comes out in a single smooth sequence.

There are never more than three consonant sounds at the beginning of a word in English. When there are three, the first one is always /s/. For the word *scream*, the hiss for the /s/ should be begun, and held, until the back of the tongue is in position to pronounce the /k/ (so-called 'hard *c*'), which should be held in turn, until the tip of the tongue is in position to pronounce the /r/. Then the three consonants can be pronounced /skr/ as one fluent sequence.

An important principle of this book is that children should learn to look at the pattern of the whole word before beginning to sound it out. Children tend to begin sounding out from the first letter of the word, and then try to carry on by adding the sound of the next letter, and so on. This works quite well for simple words like *ran* and *pot*. However, a feature of English spelling is that it often uses two or more letters to indicate one sound, and the letters don't always appear in a helpful order. For example, in each of the following words, the child needs to look beyond the first vowel to find out how to pronounce the vowel: *star*, *stalk*, *stair*, *stale*. These are all regular spelling patterns, but in each case the 'chunk' – *-ar*, *-alk*, *-air* or *-aCe* (where C stands for any consonant) – must be identified as a whole before the child begins to sound out the word.

Children should always be encouraged to monitor each pronounced word, to check that it really is a known word, and that it makes sense in the context of the completed sentence.

Naturally, as they read, children will constantly be meeting words which they have not yet worked on in worksheets. We have to assume that they will cope with some of them by relying on analogy with what they already know. They will become used to the principle of sounding out words in chunks from the very first worksheets. From this time on, as they meet a new written word, they should be encouraged to sound out any chunk which they recognise from words already known, to see if that analogy is helpful. Often, it will be.

Introduction   7

How to use this book

Phonics for Reading contains 32 'teacher's pages' (see example opposite), with suggestions for focused teaching activities. Each teacher's page is accompanied by a worksheet which offers one way of approaching a particular issue. The teacher's pages are presented in a sequence, building up from common, regular spelling–sound relations to more complex ones.

You should use your own professional judgement to decide how frequently to introduce the teaching points, how much of any activity or worksheet to use in a single session, and whether to use the reinforcement or extension activities in addition to, or in place of, the worksheet.

There is usually a wide spread of reading ability among children in a class at the beginning of year 2. Some children will be well on the way to reading independently and will be fully able to participate, not only in the introductory session with the teacher, but also in using worksheets and extension activities. Others, at an earlier stage of reading competence, will find the content, even of the simpler worksheets, quite demanding and will profit from spending a good deal of time on the preliminary activities suggested in the Teaching activities section. Some children will not yet be at a stage where they can undertake any of the worksheet alone, but may nonetheless benefit from working in the support of a group, and beginning to understand how words are chunked.

It is important to ensure that children have a secure grasp of the point in a particular worksheet or teaching session before going on to a new point. If some children still feel insecure at the end of a session, spend a second session on reinforcement and consolidation activities to lay that grounding firmly.

One very important consideration when teaching phonics is that children must recognise and understand the words which they are working with (i.e. recognise them as words which *mean* something!). The illustrative text (and picture) at the top of each worksheet are there to help to establish a context for the words. (You can substitute a suitable example from another book that the children have read if you prefer.) When doing reinforcement and extension activities, it is essential to bear in mind the need to provide a context for the words.

In working through the teaching points in the book, the children will be accumulating knowledge of a set of specific spelling–sound relationships. It is useful if they can look back and check previously taught patterns when they have difficulty with an unrecognised word. Therefore, encourage them to keep the worksheets clipped together for easy reference. To help them to find what they are looking for, each worksheet has a heading – often a simplified version of that on the teacher's page – which briefly identifies the spelling–sound regularity focused on in that worksheet.

We suggest that, in general, worksheet and extension activities are best carried out in pairs or very small groups. This is because of the complexity of the activities. While one child is sounding out and reading a word, another could be listening to the vowel sound produced by the first child to decide whether it is long or short, stressed or unstressed. Children could work together to decide, for example, whether a pair of words like *stack* and *stalk* sound the same or different.

When to use this book

The materials presented here can be used at any point from year 2 to year 4 (and upwards), depending on the individual child's reading development. (For older readers, working with texts aimed at younger readers is not a problem if the books are used as a data-base of words in context rather than for serious reading.)

Children are ready to use this book if they can:

- recognise all the letters of the alphabet, in both upper and lower case forms (A, a) and in different fonts (a, *a*);
- understand that capital letters mark the beginning of a sentence, and indicate the names of people and places;
- use basic sight vocabulary confidently;
- feel secure in using single letter–sound relationships in word-building;
- understand the difference between a 'vowel' letter and a 'consonant' letter.

If children have completed the worksheets in the Teacher's Book for the Becoming a Reader phase of **Cambridge Reading**, they should be in a good position to move on to what is offered here. An initial assessment sheet is provided which will help you to judge for yourself whether or not a child is ready.

It is important, too, that children feel comfortable with *writing* words. This is because we all appear to learn word patterns better if we lay down memories of different ways of experiencing them. A toddler first experiences words in the spoken form alone, used in meaningful contexts. As children learn to read, they need to learn to associate the written form of a word with the familiar pronounced form. Memory of the visual shape of the word on the page can be reinforced by associating with it the movements which give rise to that written form. Copying, free writing and tracing all help to establish the familiar visual patterns which are associated with the way a particular word is written.

This number refers both to the teacher's page and to the corresponding worksheet.

Number (1) or (2) means that this teacher's page and worksheet should be used in conjunction with the preceding/ following one.

What the children should learn during the session(s).

24 Verb forms with -*ed* (1)

Main learning objective

For children to recognise the suffix -*ed* at the end of words, and for them to identify the base word when they read the -*ed* form.

Supporting text
The Big Shrink
Rosemary Hayes
Picture and text from page 18

Where appropriate, answers to worksheet tasks and practical tips for using the worksheet.

The **Cambridge Reading** (Towards Independence) book from which the text extract on the worksheet is taken. The same book can be used in some of the teaching activities.

Teaching activities

- Use these activities in conjunction with teacher's page 25, which deals with -*ed* forms of base words which end in -*y*.
- Re-read a book to or with the children (e.g. *The Big Shrink*), listing the words which end in the suffix -*ed*. As you do so, ask the children to read each one, and point out that after a *t* or *d* the -*ed* ending is sounded (pronounced /id/). In all other cases the vowel is not sounded at all.
- Choose words from the list where -*ed* is added to the base form without modification (e.g. *add, ask, call, cheer*). Ask the children what each word would be if the -*ed* ending were removed.
- Move on to words ending in a consonant + *e* where only -*d* is added (e.g. *arrive, bounce, change, dance, hate*). Again, ask the children what the word would be without the ending. (Remind them that some of the verbs end in magic -*e*, and it is important that they recognise this when they look at the *ed* forms so that they know how to pronounce the vowel.)
- Repeat this with words which end in one vowel and one consonant. Show them that the consonant is doubled before -*ed* is added (e.g. *chat, drag, hop, grin*).

The worksheet

- The cloze passage on the worksheet is taken from *The Big Shrink*, so children who have access to this book could check their answers by looking at pages 10–11. The missing words are: *scuttled, seemed, pulled, squeaked, blinked, rubbed, muttered*.
- Check that the children can read the words on the worksheet aloud, making sure in particular that they do not pronounce the -*ed* as an extra syllable unless it follows *t* or *d*.

Reinforcement and extension

- The children could collect more examples of words ending in the -*ed* suffix and record them on a chart. This should be divided into columns according to how the suffix is added (i.e. 'Add *ed*', 'Double the consonant and add *ed*', 'Add *d*'). After a week, the children should note which column contains the most words.

Suggested ways to introduce the main teaching point. This is not intended to be a prescriptive sequence, and the activities can be adapted to suit the needs of a particular group of children.

For some children this work may be completed in one session, while for others it may be more appropriate to introduce the idea in one session and reinforce it in a second.

Activities to reinforce understanding for less confident children or to extend and consolidate the understanding of more confident children.

Many of these activities are games, or investigations which can continue over a week or more.

Introduction 9

Spelling and pronunciation

Fixed letter patterns

We are using the term 'fixed letter patterns', like the term 'chunk', in an informal way. Basically, we take the initial consonant(s) in a word as one fixed letter pattern, and the rest of the word as a further fixed letter pattern (e.g. *str – ange, th – ick, sp – end*). Often it is helpful to make a further analysis of the spelling pattern of 'the rest of the word' (called the 'rime'). So, in the case of *strange*, we might usefully note (i) that the rime *-ange* contains a fixed letter pattern where 'magic *-e*' indicates that the vowel written *a* is pronounced as /ei/ and (ii) that the fixed letter pattern *-ge* means that this *g* is pronounced as a 'soft g' (like the sound at the beginning and end of *judge*).

We spend a good deal of time in exploring fixed letter patterns in word-initial consonants (e.g. *wr-, sh-, kn-*) and in consonants at the end of rimes (e.g. *-ck, -ght, -tch*). Nonetheless, because there is a constant interaction of the effects of consonants on vowels, and vowels on consonants, we must also pay careful attention to vowels.

Short vowels and long vowels

There is a basic distinction, among stressed vowels, between 'short vowels' and 'long vowels'. Short vowels are those which must be followed by a consonant when they appear in words of one syllable: *pat, pet, pit, pot, putt, put* (not all accents distinguish between *putt* and *put*). The main characteristic of the remaining vowels (those in *bee, bay, buy, boy, bough, tow, two, beer, bare, bar, bore, boor, burr*) is that they are all longer than the members of the set of short vowels, so we shall refer to them as 'long vowels', even though they do not make up a homogeneous set. They include vowels which are pronounced in most accents as diphthongs (e.g. those in *now, boy, sigh*) as well as vowels which are pronounced in some accents with a final /r/ (e.g. those in *car, bear, ear*). Few aspects of pronunciation vary more between different accents than the precise phonetic quality of the long vowels. For the purposes of this book, we need only note the basic difference between short and long vowels (which is found in all accents).

Stressed and unstressed syllables

Each English word of more than one syllable has major stress on one of the syllables. The remaining syllable(s) in most short words will be unstressed. In our corpus, the majority of such words have two syllables, and have stress on the first syllable, giving a stress pattern 'DUMdi', as in:

la_dder_   f_oo_lish
br_ing_ing   h_a_ppy
c_o_ver

In each case, the vowel of the first syllable is pronounced with its full value. However, the vowel of the second syllable is much reduced and sounds either like a rather weak /i/ as in /hapi/ (*happy*), or is the nondescript weak vowel called 'shwa' – /ə/ as in /ladə/ (*ladder*). (Note that if you speak an /r/-pronouncing accent, you will pronounce the word /ladər/, keeping the same stress pattern.)

Unstressed syllables sound quieter, shorter and less clear than stressed syllables. They are more likely to disappear when you are speaking rapidly. This is true, too, of grammatical words, which are often unstressed in the stream of speech (like the *of* in 'the fifth of November').

There are many two-syllable words in the corpus which have the stress pattern 'diDUM', as in:

acr_oss_   prep_are_
beg_in_   ret_urn_
expl_ore_

Many (but not all) of such words begin with regular prefixes which are normally unstressed (e.g. *be-, ex-, pre-, re-*). It is helpful for readers, as they gain independence, to be able to recognise such prefixes and to treat them holistically, knowing that they should be unstressed when read aloud.

If you want to pronounce a word of more than one syllable, it is crucial to know which syllable receives the major stress. There is a small set of words (about 100) in English where the difference between noun and verb is marked by which syllable is stressed:

Noun	Verb
c_on_test	cont_est_
pr_o_ject	proj_ect_
t_or_ment	torm_ent_
_up_set	ups_et_

However, far more important than that, is that one way of laying down words in memory is to lay them down under their stress patterns. For instance, small children, who are just learning to speak, regularly miss out one or two unstressed syllables but always get the stressed syllable right, with pronunciations like:

/<u>na:</u>nə/   (banana)
/<u>ef</u>ən/   (elephant)
/<u>ma:</u>do/   (tomato)

If you hear a word that is stressed incorrectly, you will probably fail to recognise it. It is the stress pattern of a word which forms the basis of its aural profile.

This is obviously important for the young reader. The whole point of sounding out words is to enable children to relate the pronunciation of the spelling pattern to an existing aural/oral word form laid down in memory. If the child pronounces a spelling pattern with the wrong stress pattern, the outcome will not correctly match the remembered aural form of the word, and the child will not be able to recognise the intended word.

'Grammatical words'

It is important to teach children to recognise the written form of common grammatical words. These are short words like *that*, *where* and *have* which occur very frequently, but which children often have difficulty in learning to identify. We do not provide worksheets dealing with this issue, because the main problem does not appear to lie in the spelling/sounding-out relationship. We do, however, make some simple suggestions in this section about how teachers could approach this problem.

It is helpful to distinguish 'grammatical words' from 'content words'. Most content words are nouns, verbs or adjectives. For many of the content words in our corpus, you could draw a picture to illustrate the meaning. For instance, among nouns, you could draw an illustration to show the meaning of *armour*, *baby*, *bag*, *banana*, *beach*, *bird*, *cat*, *cake*, *line*, *lips*, *pebbles*, *ruler*, *scissors* and hundreds of others. Among verbs, you could illustrate *to bark*, *build*, *climb*, *cook*, *drive*, *give*, *iron*, *lick*. Among adjectives, you could illustrate *angry*, *big*, *green*, *little*, *colourful*, *excited*, *pretty*.

Children typically find content words much easier to remember than grammatical words, just because they are meaningful. *Tyrannosaurus* may have an unusual and difficult spelling, but many children will find it easier to recognise securely on a subsequent reading than a grammatical word like *what*. The reason seems to be that there is a very specific meaning associated with the content word *Tyrannosaurus*. The written form of the word immediately conjures up the specific meaning which the child knows very well.

The problem with *grammatical* words is that they don't have memorable meanings. Since they can occur in any sentence, their meanings are hard to pin down (impossible to draw a picture of) and they change in different contexts. For instance, the pronouns *I*, *you*, *he*, *she*, *it*, *we*, *they*, etc., refer to somebody or something different in every different conversation, depending on who is doing the talking and what they're talking about.

Grammatical words include:

- words indicating spatial relations: *in*, *out*, *up*, *down*, *here*, *there*, *this*, *that*, *near*, *beside*;
- conjunctions: *and*, *but*, *if*, *though*, *besides*;
- question words: *who*, *what*, *where*, *when*, *why*, *how*;
- common little verbs: *is*, *are*, *was*, *were*, *have*, *had*, *can*, *might*, *should*, *would*, *do* (you can tell which ones are grammatical verbs by whether or not they can add the contracted form of the negative as in *isn't*, *can't*, *don't*, *shouldn't*, *haven't*, *mustn't*, etc.).

One striking feature of these words is that they are short. Most of them consist of only one syllable. A second feature is that they occur astonishingly frequently in texts. One or more of them occurs in almost every sentence you look at. In our corpus of just over 40,000 items,

> *the* occurs 2400 times
> *and* occurs 1243 times
> *they* occurs 410 times
> *but* occurs 263 times
> *that* occurs 256 times.

Between them, grammatical words account for nearly half of all the words in our corpus (over 19,000 words are grammatical words).

Ninety or more per cent of all the words beginning with *th-* or *wh-* that you meet in a text will be grammatical words:

> *the*, *that*, *their*, *them*, *then*, *there*, *these*, *they*, *this*, *those*
> *what*, *when*, *where*, *whether*, *which*, *while*, *who*, *whose*, *why*

Children often find the similar look of the written form of these two sets of words particularly confusing. It may be helpful to teach these words in small sets, exploring their meaning and contexts of use, so that children have some explicit notions of meaning to attach to particular forms. For instance, the question words *who*, *which*, *when*, *where*, *why* could be taught as a set (together with *how*), drawing attention to the *wh-* spelling. The class could generate sets of questions about a story using these words, and writing them down.

In another lesson, the relationships *here* (near me) and *there* (over there) could be compared with *this* (*one*) (near me) and *that* (*one*) (over there) in a game which involves pointing to near and distant objects and places, drawing attention to their *th-* spelling patterns. At a later time, children could undertake an activity which shows the way the set *here*, *there*, *where* is concerned with location in space, whereas *when* and *then* are concerned with time. The point of each activity would be to try to associate particular meanings and contexts of use with the familiar spoken forms and the unfamiliar written forms of each word.

A feature of many grammatical words is that they can be pronounced as contracted forms, which are represented in the spelling with apostrophes. We have already mentioned that grammatical verbs may have attached negative forms (e.g. *isn't, don't, wouldn't, can't*) but there are many other grammatical contracted forms: *I'm, we're, he's, they've, I'd, she'll, let's, could've*, etc. No content words can be contracted.

It seems likely that a contributory reason for children having particular difficulty in remembering the written form of grammatical words is because many grammatical words have a number of different pronunciations, depending on whether or not they are stressed, and whether they occur in a contracted form. Evidence for some confusion among the written forms of grammatical words is often found in children's early attempts at writing where, for instance, the spoken expression /kudəv/ (where the second syllable is unstressed) is often written out as *could of* rather than as *could have*.

For many children, grammatical words are the hardest words to learn to identify. Yet every second word in a text is likely to be one of the common hundred or so grammatical words. Moreover, they play an important role in indicating the relationships between words in the sentence. There is real sense in saying that, although they carry so little independent meaning, these are the most important words for a child to learn to read accurately and confidently.

English spelling – some background

There are many reasons why English spelling is as complex as it is:

- We still use a basically Latin form of alphabet which has only five vowel symbols (*a, e, i, o, u*) because Latin was a language with relatively few different vowel qualities which could be comfortably written with only five vowel symbols (and *y*). English, in contrast, has up to 24 vowel sounds, depending on the accent you speak. These all have to be written with only five vowel symbols. In fact, we also use *r, w, y* and *l* (e.g. *par, paw, pay, palm*) as well as devices like consonant doubling (e.g. *later/latter*), to write vowels. But that means we have had to construct *combinations* of letters to represent all the pronounced vowels, and it is the number and variety of these combinations which take years for learners to master.

- People have been writing some form of English for well over a thousand years, and during that period the spoken language has undergone many changes which are not always reflected in the spelling. Spelling tends to be conservative (e.g. the initial *k-* in words like *knee, knight, knock* and *know* has not been pronounced in English for nearly four hundred years).

- English has borrowed words from many different languages and often preserves the spelling equivalents of the language of origin, rather than writing them as they are pronounced in English (e.g. the initial *p-* in words like *psychology* or *pneumonia* has never been pronounced in English).

- English has developed many different accents over the last 1,500 years. It was first written down by scribes who lived in different parts of the country and spoke with different accents. Each scribe would try to represent his own pronunciation in the written form, which did not become fully standardised until well into the nineteenth century. Modern English spelling still retains traces of this ancestry of differing accents. Many of its curiosities do actually still make sense in one or other of the accents still spoken in the British Isles. You can still, for instance, find Scottish speakers who pronounce a short vowel and a guttural consonant before the /t/ in *right* and other *-ight* words, making it sound quite different from *rite*.

Unfortunately for beginning readers, variation in spelling–sound relationships is particularly obvious in the most commonly used words, which have been in the language for hundreds of years. We see different spelling–sound patterns when we compare long-established words like:

do/so
that/what
were/where
own/down
through/though.

In each pair, the same spelling pattern indicates different spoken vowel qualities (for many speakers of English).

However, once the frequently occurring oddities of common grammatical words in English have been learned, and learned they have to be, there are regularities in spelling–sound relationships which yield generalisations which are often more than 85% reliable. We shall concentrate in this book on generalisations which have a good reliability yield.

Accents

Speakers from different areas may speak with different accents. For speakers of different accents, there are different relationships between some spelling patterns and sounds.

We list below just a few of the well-known features which differ between accents. (See how many you share.) There are many speakers in different regions who rhyme (or pronounce exactly the same) both words in each of the following pairs:

boot – foot   (northern England and Scotland)
but – put   (Midlands, Lancashire and Yorkshire)
bird – bud   (London Jamaican)
poor – paw   (Midlands and south-east)
finger – singer   (Midlands)
mass – pass   (northern England, west England, Scotland, USA)
bomb – balm   (USA)
cot – caught   (Scotland)
where – wear   (most of England)

However, for every accent that does rhyme one of these pairs of words (and others with the same vowel and consonant pattern), there are many others which do not.

Initial *h-*

Speakers of most English accents do not, in normal current speech, pronounce the initial /h/ in grammatical words like *have*, *had*, *here*, *him*, *her*. Many speakers, particularly speakers of urban accents, will also not pronounce the /h/ in words like *happen*, *home*, *house*, *Harry*, *behave*. In sounding out spelling patterns, we believe that children should learn to sound the /h/ when it occurs at the beginning of a word or syllable (even if, when they repeat the whole word, they pronounce it without the /h/). The reason why we believe that it may be helpful to learn to sound the /h/ consistently is that so many common words are distinguished in spelling by the presence or absence of *h*:

is/his   *all/hall*
as/has   *it/hit*
and/hand   *ear/hear*, etc.

We are not suggesting that children should be being taught to speak 'properly' in reading sessions. We are simply suggesting that *h-* should be recognised in spelling, and pronounced during the sounding-out phase.

Accent variation and the teaching of phonics

It is particularly important for teachers to be aware of accent differences when teaching reading. Problems may arise for children learning to read if the teacher speaks an accent very different from that spoken by their pupils. For example, a child who pronounces the /r/ at the end of *flower* and in the middle of *curly* may simply not recognise a familiar word like *car* when it is pronounced by the teacher without an /r/ and spoken out of context. On the other hand, a non-/r/-pronouncing child may try to adjust to an /r/-pronouncing accent spoken by the teacher, and produce a form like *door* with a strongly pronounced /r/ at the end, which seems to be learnt as an alternative to the child's normal pronunciation without an /r/. It is not certain that, for the child, these different sound patterns represent the same word (an area ripe for research).

This is an issue which should be taken seriously, since it is possible that a major problem for many children learning to read is that they speak a different accent from their teacher. This is clearly an issue which demands a good deal of sensitivity on the part of the teacher. It may be helpful, where a teacher is aware of an accent mismatch, for the teacher to try to mimic the child's pronunciation when individual words are being pronounced out of context. It is hard enough for children to learn to read, without having, at the same time, to learn the teacher's accent.

It is because of our concern with the issues discussed in this section that we will sometimes indicate variation in spelling–sound relationships in the teacher's pages which follow. However, we will only indicate a fraction of the possible variations, and these will be between accents which we happen to know something about. We hope, however, that the fact of these occasional reminders will draw teachers' attention to the possibility of mismatches between the teacher's accent and the child's. The crucial point in the sounding-out of a word is that children should recognise the spoken form of a word as a familiar word, known to them in their own pronunciation.

Glossary

All the words are glossed in a way that will be helpful to teachers explaining them to enquiring children. They are not full linguistic definitions.

base word   The form of a word without suffixes (e.g. *bounce* is the base word of *bouncing* and *bounced*; *teddy* is the base word of *teddies*).

chunk   See Introduction, page 7 ('The aims of this book').

compound word   A word made by combining two other words (e.g. *some + where = somewhere*; *bed + room = bedroom*).

contraction / contracted form   The form generated when two words are pronounced together, leaving out or altering part of one of the words (e.g. *I am = I'm*; *will not = won't*).

fixed letter pattern   A group of letters which, when they appear together in a given pattern, are regularly pronounced in a very limited number of ways.

monosyllable   A word with one syllable (e.g. *but*, *lamb*).

polysyllable   A word with two or more syllables (e.g. *although*, *sensible*).

prefix   A fixed letter pattern which occurs at the beginning of a word and is typically unstressed, especially in verbs (e.g. *re-* in *return*; *dis-* in *discover*).

rime   The part of the word that remains after the initial consonant(s) is removed (e.g. *-ange* in *strange* and *-en* in *pen*).

shwa   The unstressed vowel at the end of words like *sofa* and at the beginning of words like *about*.

stress   See Introduction, pages 10–11.

suffix   An ending added to a base word to show a change in, for example, tense or number (see examples for **base word**).

vowels (short vowel / long vowel)   See Introduction, page 10.

PART TWO:

Teacher's pages and worksheets

1 Assessment

Main objective

To assess whether children have the necessary basic knowledge to benefit from the activities in this book. Specifically, to check whether the children:

- know and recognise short vowels;
- can read single consonants as well as consonant letter strings at the beginning of words;
- are confident in word building with simple CVC (consonant–vowel–consonant) words;
- can identify rhyming words.

Teaching activities

- Observe the children as they complete the following activities, noting how confidently they perform the tasks and whether they have any particular problems.
- Give the children some word endings (e.g. *-an*, *-at*, *-ip*) and ask them to suggest consonants which you could put in front of each ending to make a word (make sure the children are familiar with the word 'consonant'). It is important that you always write out the words the children suggest and ask the children to read them aloud.
- Show the children some initial consonants (e.g. *m*, *t*, *b*) and offer them some possible endings (e.g. *-at*, *-ap*, *-et*, *-og*, *-in*) with which they can make words. These activities will help to demonstrate whether the children are confident in word-building with simple CVC words.
- Give the children a three-letter word with the middle vowel missed out (e.g. p _ n, s _ t, b _ d) and ask the children to suggest vowels to make a word. Help them to compile a list of the five letters of the alphabet which are vowels. (Check they understand the concept of vowels – if they have difficulty with it, take them into the playground to shout words like *cat*, *bed*, *pit*, *dog*, *cub*. The sound they shout on is the vowel, e.g. ca–a–a–a–at, be–e–e–e–ed!)

The worksheet

- Ask the children to complete the first and then the second group of crosswords. Make sure that they understand that they have to make proper words reading both across and down. (For some children it may be appropriate to enlarge the crosswords and provide small squares of paper, each with a vowel written on, for children to physically move around and 'try out' before they write the letters down.)
- Ask them to write down the completed words in the spaces provided, and to read aloud all the words that they write.
- The final section of the worksheet enables you to check that the children are secure with rhyme. Do a few similar examples together first to make sure that the children understand what they have to do.

Reinforcement and extension

- See if the children can find any words that do not contain a vowel letter. This will alert them to the importance of vowels in words (though some children may eventually suggest words with *y* in them, e.g. *sky*, *try*).
- Ask the children to make up more three-letter crosswords for their friends.
- When they have worked on a number of these crosswords, let them work out which consonants can occur as single letters at the end of CVC words and which ones cannot.

Vowel crosswords

1 Name _____ Date _____

Fill in the vowels to make words.

	l				b				b				h				m	
s		t		c		n		s		n		r		b		h		m
	g				d				t				p				x	

Write the words you made. Then read them.

☐ ☐ ☐ ☐ ☐
☐ ☐ ☐ ☐ ☐

Now fill in the vowels to make more words.

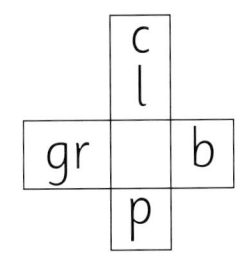

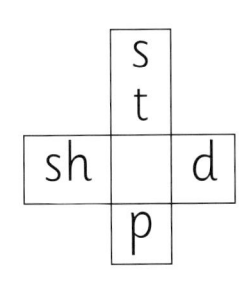

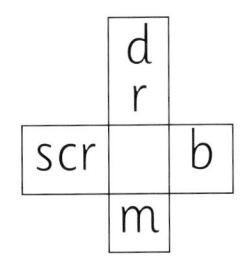

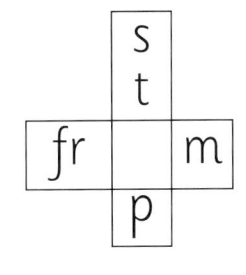

	c				s				d				s				c	
	l				t				r				t				h	
gr		b		sh		d		scr		b		fr		m		sl		p
	p				p				m				p				n	

Write the words you made. Then read them.

☐ ☐ ☐ ☐ ☐
☐ ☐ ☐ ☐ ☐

Join the words that rhyme.

leg   mat

cat   peg

bun   top

sit   fun

mop   hit

© Cambridge University Press 1997

2 Counting syllables

Main learning objective

For children to understand that words are made up of syllables. Being able to break words down in this way makes unknown words easier to handle.

> **Supporting text:**
> *Jumble Power*
> Rosemary Hayes
> Picture and text from page 23

Teaching activities

- Choose one of the children's names and tap out the syllables, preferably on a percussion instrument such as a drum. Repeat with the names of other children, with different numbers of syllables.
- Play a game by tapping a number of syllables and having all the children with that number of syllables in their name stand up, rub their heads, stand on one leg, etc.
- You could play a version of 'I Spy', using the number of syllables in the word as a clue instead of the initial letter.
- The children could form a 'syllable band'. Divide them into groups and give each group a word or phrase with a different number of syllables based on a theme (e.g. a 'winter' theme could yield *cold, snowflakes, snowy day, woolly jumper,* etc.). The children then tap out (or whisper) their words in time with each other and the other groups. This activity helps children to listen carefully to the number of syllables in words.

Note: The number of syllables in some words will vary depending on whether they are enunciated slowly and clearly or are in running speech (e.g. *chocolate* can be said with three syllables but is more often pronounced with two).

Reinforcement and extension

- Once the children have completed the worksheet, they could think of more food words to add to the three plates.
- Working in groups, the children could look through a book they are familiar with, trying to find a target number of words with one, two, three or four plus syllables. Which target do they achieve first, and are there any they cannot achieve?

Counting syllables

2 Name _____ Date _____

Casseroles, sausages, cakes, fish and chips, pizzas, hot dogs, ice-creams and a chocolate mousse all flew out of the machines and landed on the table.

Read these food names aloud.
If they have one syllable, circle them in red.
If they have two syllables, circle them in blue.
If they have three syllables, circle them in yellow.
Then put them on the right plate.

fish   ice-cream   cakes

bananas   hot dogs

chips   sausages   curry

vegetables   beefburgers

mousse   fruit

1 Syllable

2 Syllables

3 Syllables

3 Short and long vowels

Main learning objective

For children to recognise the difference between short and long vowels (see Introduction, page 10). This distinction will be fundamental to many of the activities in subsequent teacher's pages, and in particular for understanding the effect of magic -e on vowels.

> **Supporting text**
> *A Welsh Lamb*
> Richard Brown
> Picture and text from page 7

Teaching activities

- Write the words *met* and *meet* on the board. Read them aloud, emphasising the long /i:/ in *meet*. Ask the children to tell you the difference between the words, encouraging them to use the descriptions 'short' and 'long' vowels. Repeat with other pairs (e.g. *fed/feed*). The advantage of beginning with the distinction between /e/ and /i:/ is that the children can see the doubled *ee* as well as hear the longer sound.

- Introduce, orally only, other pairs of words which contrast a long and short vowel sound (e.g. *back/bake*, *hat/hate*, *kit/kite*, *lick/like*, *cot/coat*, *hop/hope*, *but/boot*, *tub/tube*). Vary whether you read the short or the long vowel version first, and ask the children to identify which is which.

- Once children are confident with these words, introduce words with long vowel sounds other than those they will encounter in learning about magic -e. As before, contrast each one with a word with a short vowel and ask the children to distinguish between them (e.g. *ton/town*, *head/heard*, *shot/short*).

Note: In accents where the pronunciation of *u* differs in *but* and *put* (see Introduction, page 13) there are six short vowel sounds rather than five.

The worksheet

- Check that the children can read all the animal names before they begin the worksheet activity. Decide together as a group where to put some of the words.

Reinforcement and extension

- Ask the children to make a set of one-syllable words on a particular theme (e.g. colours, weather words, toys, insects, flowers, things in the classroom or words related to a current class topic). Ask the children to divide the words into two groups – those with a long vowel sound and those with a short vowel sound.

- When the children have a substantial list, they could then go on to look carefully at the words with a long vowel sound to find which fixed letter patterns are associated with long vowels (see also teacher's page 7). See how many they can find.

Short and long vowels

3 Name _____ Date _____

I wanted to **keep** the **lamb** as a **pet**.

Read the words aloud.
Write the words with a short vowel sound in the short dog.
Write the words with a long vowel sound in the long dog.

fish   horse   goat   frog
bird   snake   bug   lamb   sheep
cat   mouse   wasp   fly

fish

sheep

© Cambridge University Press 1997   Original illustrations by Patricia Ludlow

4 Initial fixed letter patterns with one silent consonant

Main learning objective

For children to recognise that for some sequences of two consonants, only one sound is pronounced (e.g. *kn-*, *wh-*, *wr-*, *sc-*, *gh-*).

> **Supporting text**
> *The Pyjama Party*
> June Crebbin
> Picture and text from page 16

Teaching activities

- The children should already be familiar with words which begin with two consonants where both are pronounced (e.g. *bl-*, *br-*, *sn-*) or where the two consonants together make one new sound (e.g. *th-*, *ch-*, *sh-*). Remind them of these by eliciting examples from them (e.g. *blue, block, brush, bread, snow, sneeze* for the first group; *thick, thumb, chip, chicken, ship, shop* for the second group).
- Explain to the children that sometimes, even though two consonants are written, only one of them makes a sound. Give them some sentences containing words which demonstrate this, and ask them to find and circle the words which begin with two consonants where only one is pronounced (e.g. 'I cut with scissors and I write with a pencil'; 'My leg bends at my knee, and my arm bends at my elbow and my wrist').
- Ask them to write out the words that they found in the sentences and circle each silent letter in another colour.

Note: You could also include *wh-* words in your sentences, but note that many Scots will pronounce this as two sounds, /hw/, so for them these words should not be included.

The worksheet

- You may prefer to begin by focusing on just one fixed letter pattern, *kn-*, using the worksheet, before looking at the other examples of silent letters (i.e. *wr-*, *sc-*, *wh-*). When you go on to these others, it may be useful to make sure children have examples of these on the back of the worksheet if they are keeping the worksheets as a record to refer back to.

Reinforcement and extension

- Put up a chart on the wall, headed 'Words which begin with two consonants', and write down some example words (preferably ones that you and the children have already looked at). Divide the words into three sets, as follows:

Both pronounced	Make one new sound	Only one pronounced
step	them	wrong
climb	thought	know
Spike	chewed	ghost
bring	sheets	when
		who

Ask the children to add words to the sets over the space of a week. At the end of this period, read the words on the chart with the children and list the fixed letter patterns at the beginning of words in each group. Which set has the greatest variety of fixed letter patterns?

- Ask the children to use dictionaries to make a list of two-consonant fixed letter patterns where both are pronounced at the beginnings of words. They could do the same for three-consonant patterns (e.g. *scr-*, *spr-*, *str-*).

Silent consonants at the beginning of words

4 Name _____ Date _____

The pillow **kn**ocked a jug of flowers.

Make words by adding **kn** to these word endings.
Then write the words under the pictures.

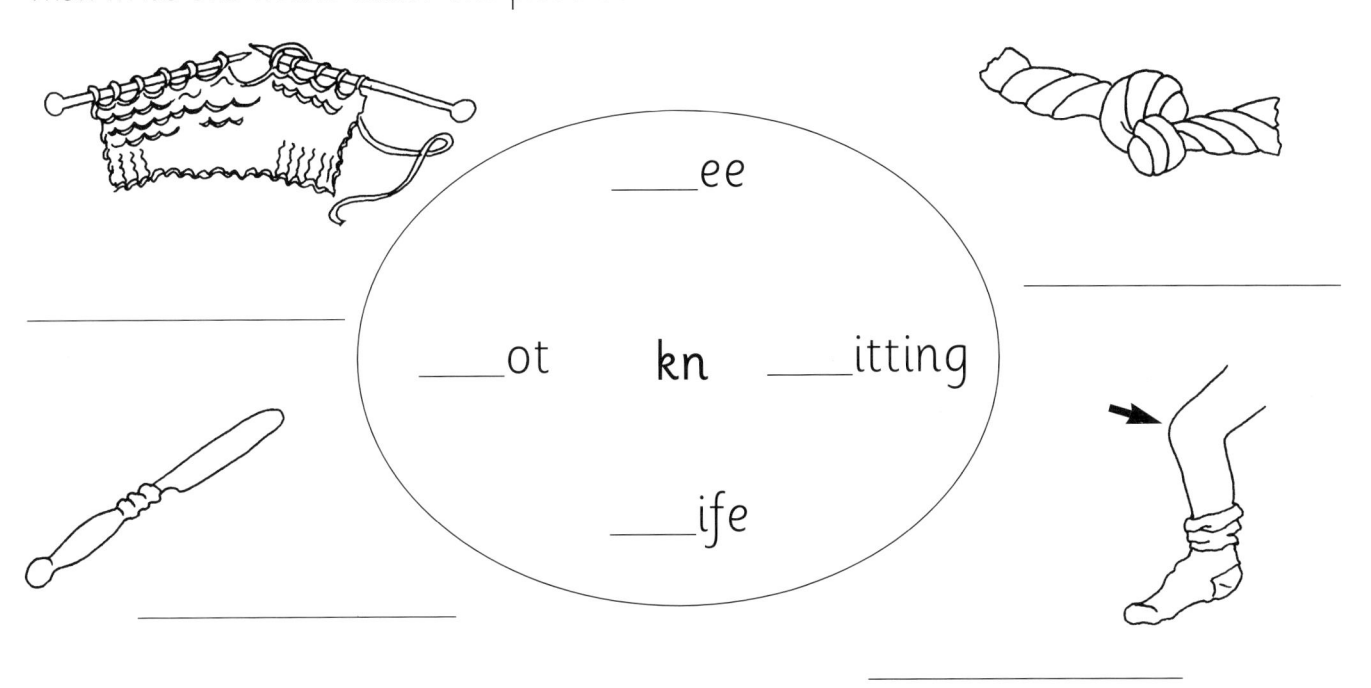

___ee

___ot   kn   ___itting

___ife

Use the words to fill in the gaps.

Grandma was _____ a jumper for Emma's present.

Emma fell over and hurt her _____ .

The _____ in the string was too tight for Emma to untie it,

so Dad cut it with a sharp _____ .

Look in your dictionary and find more words which begin with **kn-** .

© Cambridge University Press 1997   Original illustrations by Peter Kavanagh

5 Hard and soft c

Main learning objective

For children to recognise that when *c* is followed by *e* or *i*, it is softened to /s/.

> **Supporting text**
> *Spike and the Concert*
> June Crebbin
> Picture and text from page 17

Teaching activities

- Look together at the title of *Spike and the Concert*. Draw the children's attention to the word *concert*, asking them to focus on the two *c*s. Can the children describe the difference in sound quality between them?
- Introduce the terms 'hard *c*' (as in *car*, *collar*, *second*, *traffic*, *music*) and 'soft *c*' (as in *centre*, *city*, *mice*, *palace*, *decide*). Write some words and ask them to classify the *c* in each word as hard or soft, underlining hard *c*s in one colour and soft *c*s in another.
- Ask the children if they can detect the fixed letter patterns which include soft *c*, i.e. which vowel follows *c* when it is pronounced /s/. They should observe that *ce* and *ci* generate soft *c*.
- Ask them to check whether any of the words with hard *c* feature the fixed letter patterns *ce* or *ci*.

The worksheet

- Most of the words on the worksheet are taken from *Spike and the Concert*, so when the children have finished the worksheet they could add to the lists by hunting for more examples in the same book.

Reinforcement and extension

- Encourage the children to investigate fixed letter patterns which generate soft *g* (as in *germs*, *gentle*, *giant*, *giraffe*, *cage*, *orange*, *magic*, *register*). They should find a remarkable similarity to those which generate soft *c* – but note that there are many more exceptions (e.g. *get*, *give*, *giggle*, *girl*, *stronger*, *forget*). The lesson to be learned from this is that, while awareness of generalisations is very helpful in determining the possible alternatives, there is no substitute for listening to what you read and making sure you read sense!
- Ask the children to find other fixed letter patterns in which *c* occurs in *Spike and the Concert*. They should come up with -*ck* as in *back*, *ch*- as in *chairs* and as in *choir*, *cl*- as in *clarinets*, *chr*- as in *Christmas*, etc.

Hard c and soft c

5 Name _____ Date _____

Mrs Fraser looked at her watch. "Well, he'll have to **c**ome with us," she de**c**ided. "We **c**an't leave him here."

Look at the words in the food bowl.
If a word has a soft **c**, as in de**c**ide, write it in the ear on the left.
If it has a hard **c**, as in **c**ome, write it in the ear on the right.

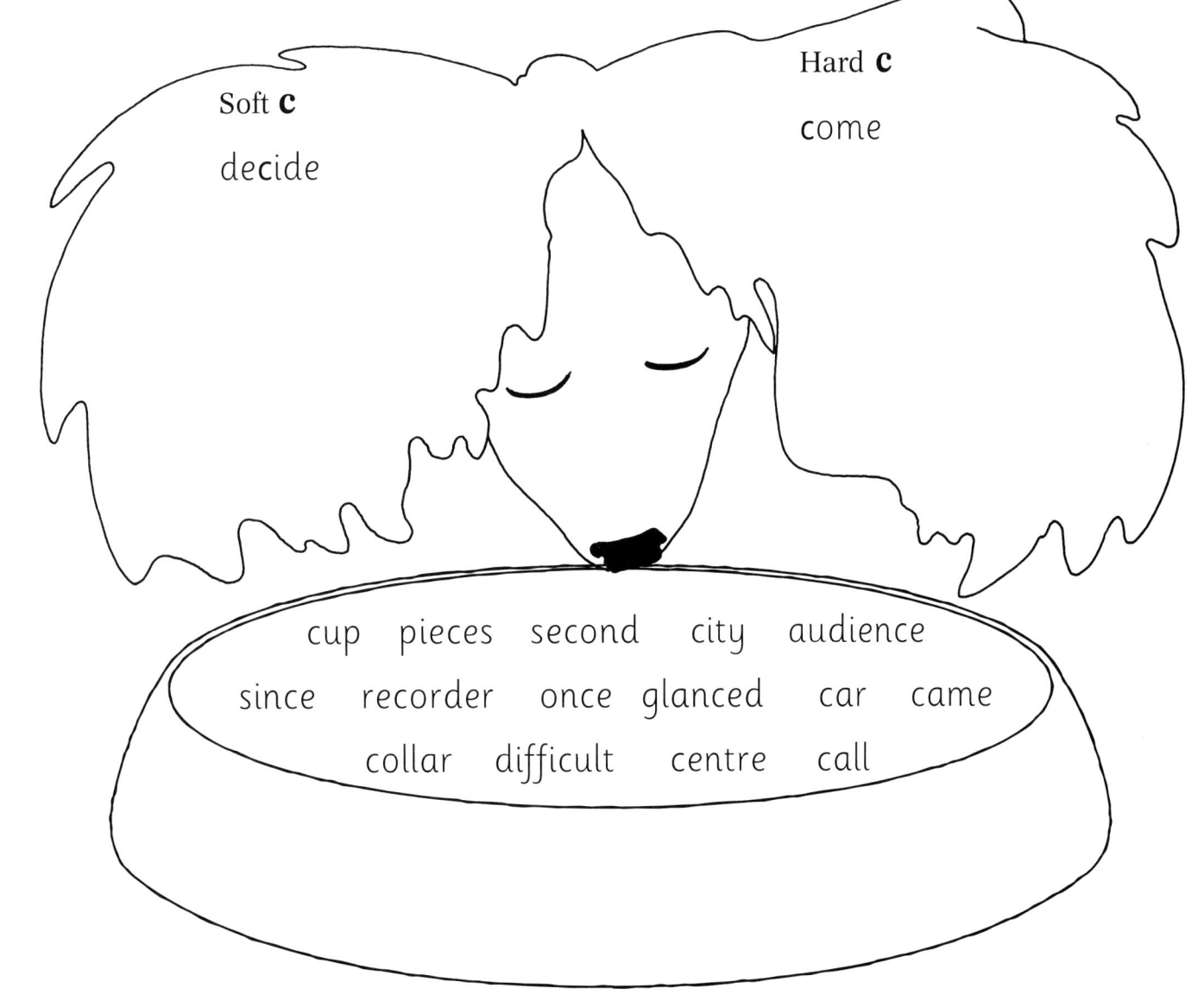

Soft **c**
decide

Hard **c**
come

cup   pieces   second   city   audience
since   recorder   once   glanced   car   came
collar   difficult   centre   call

Look at the words in the ears. Look at the vowel after the **c**.
What do you notice about the vowel after soft **c**?

© Cambridge University Press 1997   Original illustrations by Peter Kavanagh

6 Fixed letter patterns at the end of words (1)

Main learning objective

To familiarise children with some common fixed letter patterns at the end of monosyllabic words (*-tch*, *-dge*, *-ck*, *-ng*, *-nk*). Those covered in the worksheet are always preceded by short vowels – worksheet 7 will include some that can be preceded by either short or long vowels.

> **Supporting text**
> *The Big Shrink*
> *Rosemary Hayes*
> Picture and text from page 4

Teaching activities

- Write on the board a selection of monosyllabic words ending with the fixed letter patterns *-tch*, *-dge*, *-ck*, *-ng* and *-nk* (e.g. *match*, *witch*, *hedge*, *badge*, *lick*, *duck*, *bang*, *song*, *think*, *sunk*). Ask the children to read them aloud.
- Ask the children to listen hard to the vowel sounds as you re-read the words and tell you whether they are long or short.
- Look at the examples in the supporting text quotation at the top of the worksheet and at the word endings in the activity. Again, are the vowel sounds long or short?

The worksheet

The words on the worksheet are: *fetch*, *bridge*, *back*, *string*, *catch* and *shrink*.

Reinforcement and extension

- The children could make a similar worksheet for their friends using other examples of words containing the target fixed letter patterns (they could find these by looking through *The Big Shrink* or another book with which they are familiar). Their new worksheet must end with the instruction to write out the words that they have made.
- Put up a chart on the wall divided into five columns headed '*-ck*', '*-tch*', '*-dge*', '*-nk*' and '*-ng*' and ask children to add words to the list as they think of them or find them over the space of a week. At the end of the week read the words aloud with the children, encouraging them to notice that the vowel is always short before these fixed letter patterns.

Word endings (1)

6 Name _____ Date _____

Sam and Jason bumped into Mr Mulch as he was coming out to **fetch** the rest of the class.

Make words by joining a word beginning with a word ending.
You must use all the beginnings and endings.

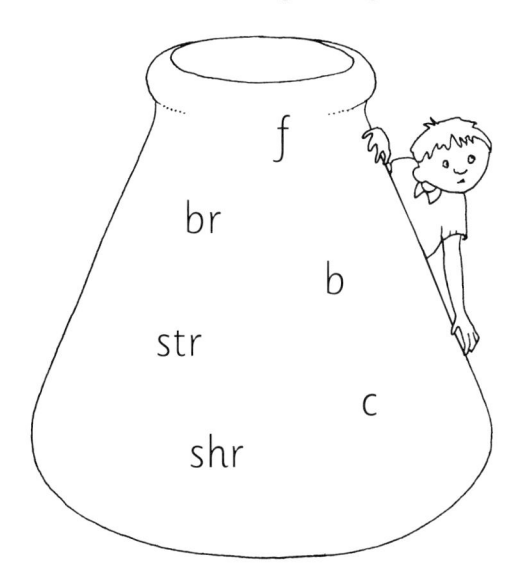

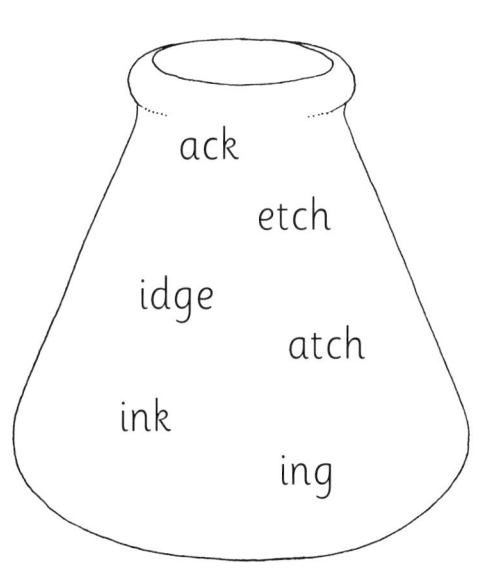

Beginnings: f, br, b, str, c, shr

Endings: ack, etch, idge, atch, ink, ing

Write the words you made. Then read them aloud.

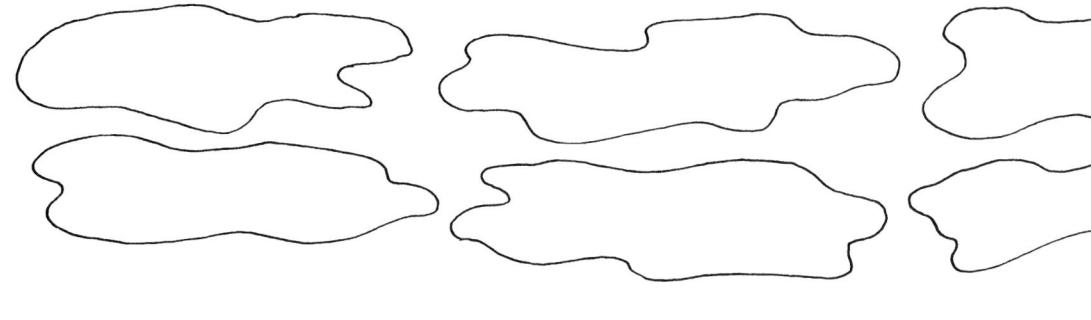

Think of six more short words with these endings and write them in the shoe.

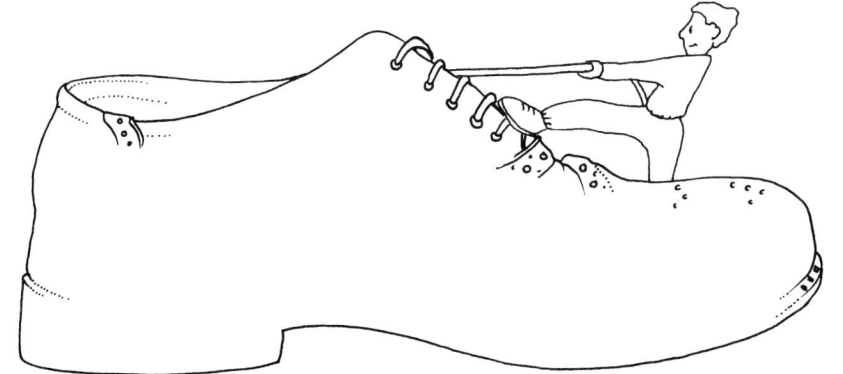

© Cambridge University Press 1997   Original illustrations by Ian Newsham

7 Fixed letter patterns at the end of words (2)

Main learning objective

To familiarise children with some further word endings (*-st, -nt, -nd, -ss*) and in particular for them to recognise that certain fixed letter patterns can be preceded by *long* vowels as well as short vowels.

> **Supporting text**
> *Mr Mulch's Magic Mixtures*
> Rosemary Hayes
> Picture and text from page 19

Teaching activities

- Remind the children of the fixed letter patterns they met in worksheet 6, which could only follow short vowels. Tell them that there are others which can follow long vowels as well as short ones.
- Write down some example words for each letter pattern. Ask the children to read the words aloud and circle the ones which contain a long vowel:

    sand, bend, find, blond
    last, best, mist, lost, post, dust
    ant, tent, pint, mint, hunt

    For some children it may be helpful to draw the long and short dogs used in worksheet 3 and to write the words on pieces of paper which children can place on the appropriate dog.

- Remind them that there is nothing obvious in the spelling to show that these vowels are long. It is therefore important to listen to the sound of the word and make sure it is a real word (demonstrate that *find*, *post* and *pint* make no sense when pronounced with a short vowel).

Note: You need to be particularly aware of how differences in regional accents may affect the activities on this page. Note especially that the *a* in words like *fast, plant, can't* and *class* may be long in some accents, particularly in southern England, and short in others. This means that, with some children, *all* the words with a final fixed letter pattern of *-ss* will have a short vowel.

Reinforcement and extension

- Give the children other fixed letter patterns and ask them to look for one-syllable words with these endings, over the space of a week:

    e.g. **-ld** (*held, field, shield, cold, build, wild, child*)
    -th (*with, earth, mouth, bath, both*)
    -ft (*left, soft, loft, tuft, lift*)
    -ch (*rich, which, each, teach, coach*)
    -sh (*wish, fish, smash, wash, fresh*)
    -sk (*ask, task, whisk, husk, musk*)
    -mp (*lamp, camp, bump, limp, dump*)
    -pt (*kept, crept*)

    The children should decide whether the vowel sound is long or short for each word.

- Ask the children to decide which vowels are most often long before the fixed letter patterns they have looked at, and which are usually short. (They should conclude that *i* and *o* are most often lengthened, plus *a* in some accents.)

Word endings (2)

7 Name _____ Date _____

"I fetched my Magic Shrink-Mix and came to **find** you," said Mr Mulch.

Read these words aloud.
If they have a long vowel, ring them with a blue pencil.
If they have a short vowel, ring them with a red pencil.

-st: most, just, fast, best, ghost

-nt: can't, plant, front, don't, sent

-ss: class, dress, kiss, moss, pass

-nd: hand, mend, find, pond, kind

© Cambridge University Press 1997   Original illustrations by Ian Newsham

8 Magic -e

Main learning objective

For children to recognise the effect of 'magic -*e*' on preceding vowels (in monosyllables). Also, to emphasise the importance of looking at the whole pattern of a word before beginning to sound it out.

> **Supporting text**
> *Dancing to the River*
> Grace Hallworth
> Picture and text from page 20

Teaching activities

- Ask a child to read aloud the words *mad* and *made*, and make sure they can hear the difference in the vowel sounds. Use the terms 'short' and 'long' vowels. Ask the children to tell you what spelling difference would account for the difference in pronunciation, and tell them that this *e* is often called 'magic -*e*'.

- Give the children some more pairs of words so that they can see whether the same pronunciation change occurs with each of the other vowels in turn (e.g. *pet/Pete, win/wine, not/note, tub/tube*).

- Explain to the children that the magic -*e* rule works only when the fixed letter pattern is 'one vowel + one consonant + *e*' (it does not necessarily apply when there are two consonants between the vowel and the *e*, as in *since, dance* and *pulse*, although it does in *paste*).

Note: When doing the activities on this page, avoid words in which the -*e* ending is preceded by *r*. Vowel + *re* will be dealt with on teacher's page 17.

Reinforcement and extension

- Ask the children to make a list of suitable words to demonstrate to each other the effect of magic -*e* on vowels. They should only use real words and, ideally, they should find pairs of words which share the same spelling apart from the magic -*e* (e.g. *cap/cape, pip/pipe, hop/hope, cut/cute*). They will find it much more difficult to find suitable words for *u–e* (e.g. *cub/cube*) and *e–e* (e.g. *scene*).

  Be aware that the children working on -*ite* (e.g. *white, write*) are likely to encounter problems, since more words end in -*ight* than in -*ite* (e.g. *right, height*). The -*ght* ending will be dealt with on teacher's page 13.

- Tell the children there are some very common words where the rule does not apply and the vowel is not lengthened. These include *have, love* and *give* (where *e* in fact simply marks the end of the word, since no proper English words end in *v*) and *some* and *come*.

Magic -e

8 Name _____ Date _____

Turtle danced faster and faster, and she m**ade** bigger and bigger steps. Watchman was trying to keep in t**ime** with Turtle.

Read the words in each turtle. Listen to the vowel sound.
Decide which sack to write each word in.

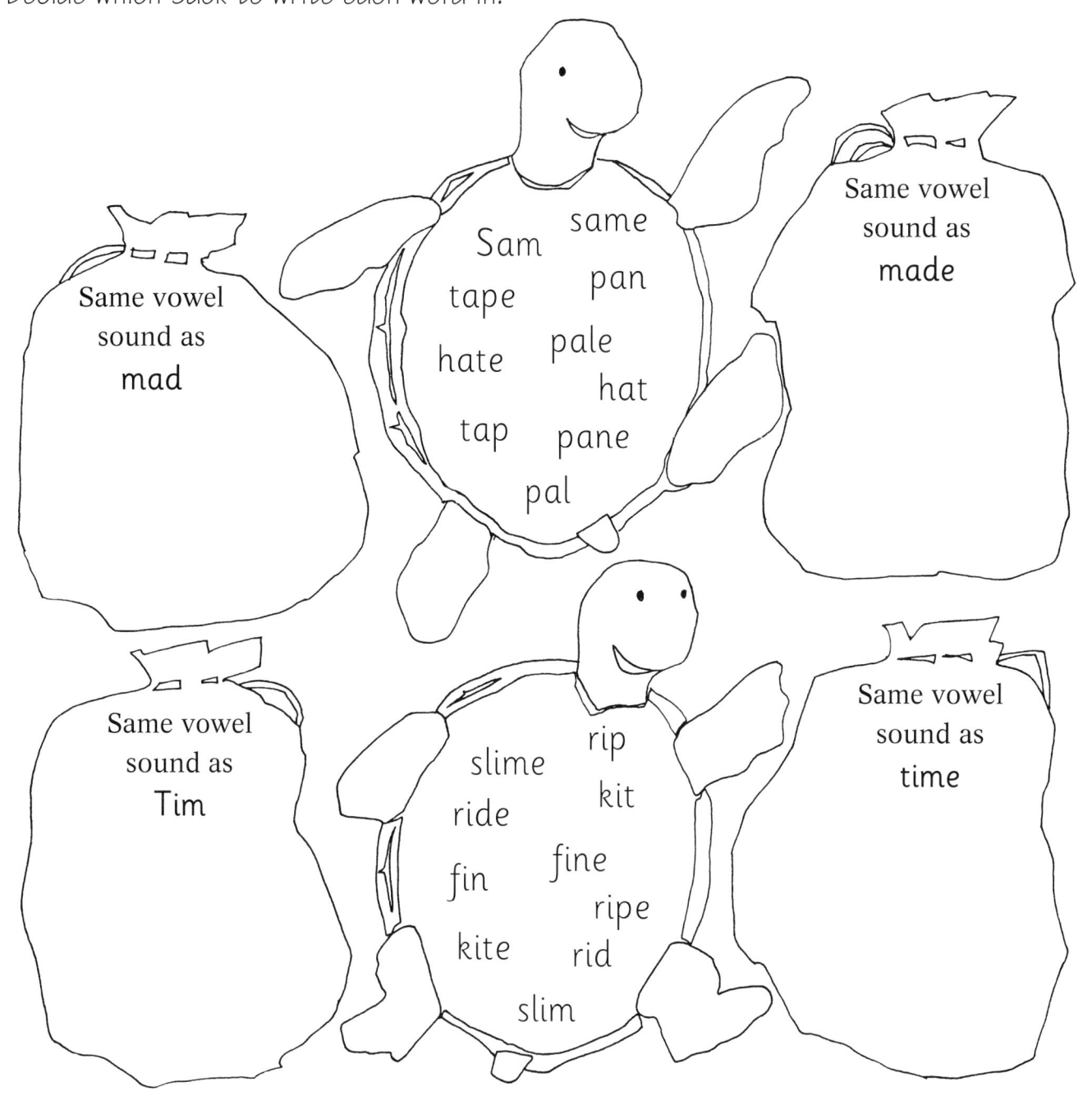

Same vowel sound as **mad**

Sam, same, tape, pan, hate, pale, hat, tap, pane, pal

Same vowel sound as **made**

Same vowel sound as **Tim**

slime, rip, ride, kit, fin, fine, ripe, kite, rid, slim

Same vowel sound as **time**

9 Fixed letter patterns *ee* and *ea*

Main learning objective

For children to recognise the fixed letter patterns *ee* and *ea* and to understand that, while *ee* has a constant pronunciation, *ea* has two main pronunciations.

> **Supporting text**
> *Mr Mulch's Magic Mixtures*
> Rosemary Hayes
> Picture and text from page 13

Teaching activities

- Show the children one or two examples of words containing the fixed letter pattern *ee* (e.g. *bee, cheese, deep, seed, wheel)* and ask them to use a picture dictionary to make a list of more examples.
- Then repeat this with *ea* words (e.g. *leaf, meat, bean, pea, seal, peace, clean, stream, beast, please, head, bread, sweat, meant*). (If some children have poor dictionary skills, it may be more appropriate to provide ready-made lists.)
- Look first at the *ee* list and ask the children how *ee* is pronounced and whether it sounds the same in all the words on their list.
- Now look at the *ea* list. Ensure that the children realise that there are two different pronunciations in this group. Divide the words according to the vowel sound – /iː/ (as in *leaf, meat, clean, please*) and /e/ (as in *bread, head, sweat*).
- Tell the children that it is their knowledge of English words that is their main clue when deciding how to pronounce a particular *ea* word. They should pronounce it in the way that makes sense. (If they come across a new word to which they cannot match a known word, *ea* usually sounds like the vowel in *bead*. They should try that first.)

The worksheet

- Before the children do the sorting activity on the worksheet, it may be helpful if you write the *ea* words on slips of paper for children to sort into the two sound groups.

Reinforcement and extension

- Tell the children that *ea* can have other pronunciations, particularly when followed by *r* (e.g. *heart; heard; pear, bear, swear, wear; beard, ear, fear, clear*). You could make an activity similar to the one on the worksheet but contrasting either words like *head* with words like *fear* and *beard*, or words like *bead* with words like *bear* and *wear*.
- You could ask the children to carry out similar activities for the fixed letter pattern *oo*. Again, there are two common pronunciations (i.e. that in *foot* and that in *boot*) and readers must rely on self-monitoring to ensure that they are reading sense. (If children meet a word they do not recognise, the pronunciation in *boot* is the more common, except before a final *-k*.) You could construct a similar trail where children have to join up '*boot*' words and '*foot*' words, or get the children to construct one for their friends.

Note: Speakers of some regional accents pronounce *oo* in the same way in *boot* and *foot*. For them, the distinguishing activity suggested above would not be relevant.

Words with -ee- and -ea-

9 Name _____ Date _____

The water was very d**ee**p and very cold. Jody's clothes were wet and h**ea**vy and it was hard to k**ee**p afloat, but at last she r**ea**ched the edge of the puddle.

I need **ee** words. Draw a yellow trail to join them up.

I want words where **ea** sounds like the **ea** in **head**. Draw a green trail to join them up.

green
bee
gleam
heavy
squeeze
head
beak
please
instead
jeans
deep
reach
feet
beans
bead
weed

I want words where **ea** sounds like the **ea** in **bead**. Draw a red trail to join them up.

© Cambridge University Press 1997   Original illustrations by Ian Newsham

10 Short vowel pronunciation of *wa-* (1)

Main learning objective

For children to begin to recognise *wa-* as a fixed letter pattern pronounced /wo/. (This includes *wha-*, *swa-*, *qua-* and *squa-*.)

> **Supporting text**
> *The Watch by the Sea*
> Richard Brown
> Picture and text from page 7

Teaching activities

- Use these activities in conjunction with teacher's page 11, which deals with *wa-* pronounced with a long vowel sound.
- Write a few simple monosyllabic words containing the letter *a* (e.g. *ant*, *cat*, *map*) but not containing *wa-*. Ask the children to read them aloud and listen to the vowel sound. Repeat with the letter *o* (e.g. *lock*, *dog*, *hot*).
- Ensure that all the children can hear the difference in sound by writing the letters *a* and *o* each on a separate piece of paper. Read some pairs of words and ask the children to point to the letter sound they can hear in each case: *hat/hot*, *sock/sack*, *pot/pat*, *map/mop*, *bag/bog*.
- Then read out the title of the book *A Watch by the Sea* and ask the children which sound they can hear in the word *watch* – is it like the vowel in *hat* or *hot*?

The worksheet

- Before the children do the worksheet, ask them to read the words aloud and tell you which set they should go in. Alternatively, play a game with the children in which you give each child a card with one of the worksheet words written on it. They then have to sort themselves into two sets according to the sound of their word.
- When the worksheet has been completed, ask the children whether there are any other vowels in any of the words (there are not). (Teacher's page 11 deals with *wa-* words which do include other vowels.)

Reinforcement and extension

- When the children have completed the worksheet, ask them to sort the words into pairs according to the consonant(s) that comes after the *a* (*has/was*, *cat/what*, *lamp/swamp*, *plan/swan*, etc.).
- The children could use a simple dictionary to find words which begin with *qu* + *a* or *squ* + *a* (e.g. *quarrel*, *squash*, *squabble*). Although there is no *w*, *qu* is pronounced /kw/ and this has the same effect on the *a* as an orthographic *w* does.
- Point out to the children that there are a small number of *wa-* words which are pronounced with the short vowel sound /a/ rather than /wo/ (e.g. *wag*, *wax*).

Words beginning with wa- (1)

10 Name _____ Date _____

When **I wa**nted to plunge my arms deep into the rock-pools, I'd take off my **wa**tch.

hat

what

Same vowel sound as hand

Same vowel sound as hop

Read each word aloud. Write it on the correct watch strap.

lamp
want
hat
what
was
clap
plan
hatch
swamp
has
swap
swan
pant
watch

Look at the words with the same vowel sound as **hop**. Which letter pattern can you see in these words?

© Cambridge University Press 1997   Original illustrations by Annabel Large

11 Long vowel pronunciation of *wa-* (2)

Main learning objective

For children to recognise the conditions under which the *a* in *wa-* is pronounced as a long vowel.

> **Supporting text**
> *Coyote Girl*
> Rosalind Kerven
> Picture and text from page 23

Teaching activities

- The children should have completed the activities on the previous teacher's page, which deals with *wa-* pronounced with a short vowel sound, before undertaking these activities.
- Ask the children to make a list of words beginning with *wa-*, using a simple picture dictionary. Ask them to pick out from the list all the words which are pronounced with a short vowel – this should confirm their understanding of the /wo/ words which they looked at in the previous worksheet.
- Their remaining list should consist only of words with a long vowel. Ask the children whether the vowel sounds the same in all the remaining words. They should notice that there are two long vowel sounds represented – that in *walk* and that in *wait*. Ask them to divide the words into two sets according to which of the two vowel sounds the words have.
- The knowledge that the vowel after *wa-* can be long or short depending on what follows can be extremely useful when attempting to sound out unrecognised words, and is another example of the need to look carefully at the pattern of the whole word before attempting any sounding out.

The worksheet

- The children should do the worksheet in pairs. They may find it useful to write the completed words on another piece of paper. One child should read the words aloud while the other listens and assigns the words to one of the pots at the bottom of the sheet.

- Ask the children if they can find any reason for the long vowels in each of the pots. They may well observe that the words in the *wait*-like set all involve other vowels, mostly magic *-e* (e.g. *wade*, *waste*, *wave*). Most of the words in the *walk*-like set involve *r* or *l*, both of which are consonants which have an effect on vowel sounds (see teacher's pages 12 and 16).

Reinforcement and extension

- The children could play this simple game:
  1. Cut up 24 small strips of paper.
  2. On each one write a word ending which could be added to *wa-* to form a monosyllabic word with: a short vowel (eight strips), a *wait*-like vowel (eight strips) or a *walk*-like vowel (eight strips).
  3. Turn the strips over so the writing cannot be seen.
  4. Three children (or pairs of children) can play. Each child/pair decides which of the three kinds of words they are going to collect (i.e. those with a short vowel, a *wait*-like vowel or a *walk*-like vowel). Give each of them a strip of paper with *wa* written on it.
  5. In turns, each child/pair turns over an ending. They try combining it with their *wa* slip, and if it makes a word in the set they are collecting, they keep it. Otherwise they turn it over and return it to its position.
  6. The first child/pair to collect all eight of their word endings wins the game.

Words beginning with **wa-** (2)

11

Name _____ Date _____

As soon as the **wa**ter was nice and **wa**rm, she told the coyote girl to jump in.

Join wa- and an ending from the large pot to make new words.

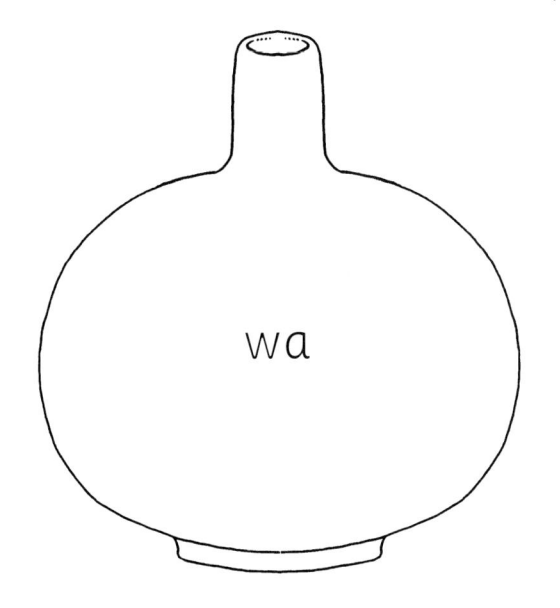

wa

ter, y, ve, rn, lk, ll, it, rm, ke, de, ste

Say the new words you made. Decide which new pot to write them in.

Words with the same vowel sound as **walk**

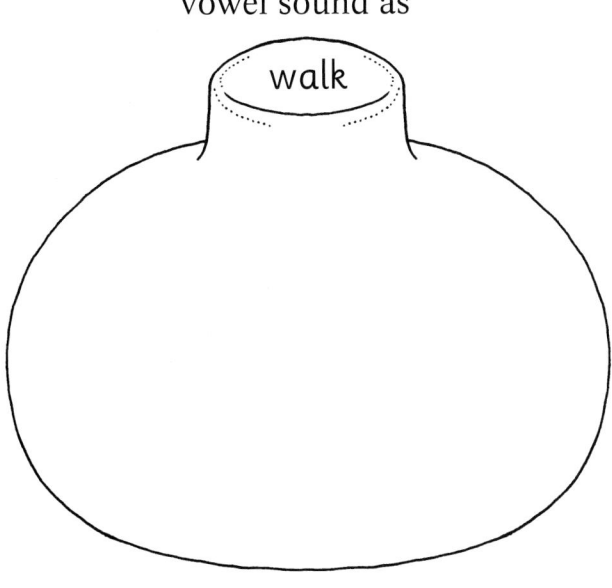

Words with the same vowel sound as **wait**

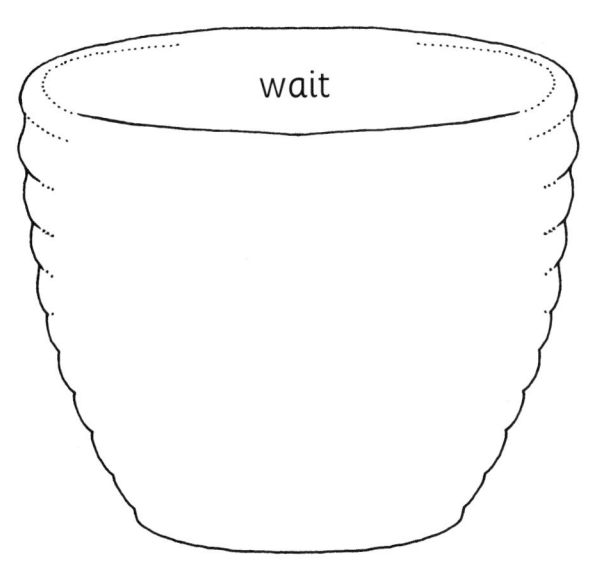

© Cambridge University Press 1997   Original illustrations by Amanda Hall

12 Vowel + *ll*

Main learning objective

For children to recognise that when *l* follows a vowel it can affect its pronunciation, and for them to recognise vowel + *ll* as a fixed letter pattern.

> **Supporting text**
> *The Dog Show*
> June Crebbin
> Picture and text from page 4

Teaching activities

- Tell the children that there are some fixed letter patterns which contain a vowel and a consonant (usually *l, r, w* or *y*) in which the consonant affects the sound of the vowel. Remind them of the *wa-* fixed letter pattern on worksheets 10 and 11.
- Re-read a book to or with the children, picking out and listing the words which end in *-ll*. Ideally, include words which contain each of the different vowels (e.g. *ball, wall, tell, well, still, will, doll, jolly, full, bull*).
- Ask the children to read the listed words aloud, listening to whether each word is pronounced with a short vowel or a long vowel. Ring the words with short vowels in one colour and those with long vowels in another.
- The children should notice that the *-all* endings are long vowels whereas the others are all short vowels. (For some southern English accents, the vowel sounds in *dull* and *full* are different. They are, however, both short vowels.)

Reinforcement and extension

- Give each child (or group of children) one of the following fixed letter patterns involving *l* + consonant, and ask them to find and list words which end in that pattern:

  -ld (e.g. *bald, held, child, wild, build, cold, told*)
  -lk (e.g. *talk, walk, elk, milk, silk, yolk, folk, sulk*)
  -lf (e.g. *half, calf, shelf, elf, wolf, golf, gulf*)
  -lt (e.g. *salt, halt, belt, melt, kilt, built, bolt, colt, adult, result*)

- When they have made a list, ask them to work out which vowels are long before their fixed letter pattern. Ask the children or groups to share what they have learnt about their fixed letter pattern, and to look at each other's lists to see which pattern generated the most words.
- Their research should lead to these conclusions:
  – *a* is a long vowel before *l* + consonant (but see note below);
  – *e* and *u* are always short vowels;
  – *i* and *o* are sometimes short and sometimes long.
- It is useful for children to remember that, when they meet an unrecognised word containing an *l* + consonant letter pattern, they may need to try pronouncing the word with a long vowel.

Note: It is important to be aware that regional accent differences may affect the length of the vowel in some of these words (e.g. the *a* in *salt* and *half* may be short, not long, in some accents where they are pronounced /solt/ and /haf/).

Vowel + ll

12 Name _____ Date _____

The bath water was soon **full** of hair. "Never mind," said Alice. "It'll **all** go down the plug-hole."

Each ◯ hides a vowel. Fill in the missing vowels.

She p◯lled out the plug. Most of the water disappeared.

Bright sunshine f◯lled the room.

Behind Alice, a sm◯ll boy started to cry.

"What a mess! Just wait t◯ll Dad sees this."

"He doesn't do what you t◯ll him."

"Hello," said the vet. "What's your dog c◯lled?"

"W◯ll done, Spike," said Jess.

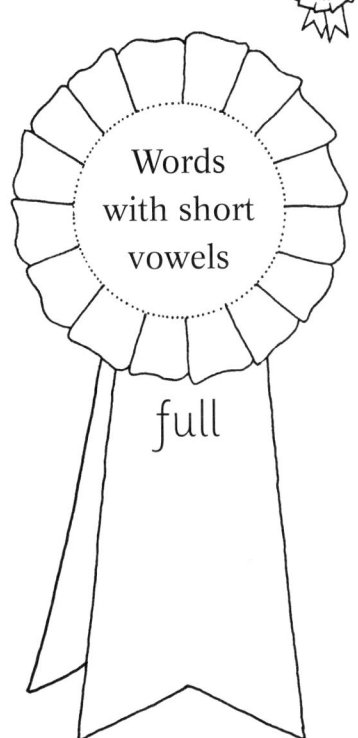

Write the words in the rosettes.

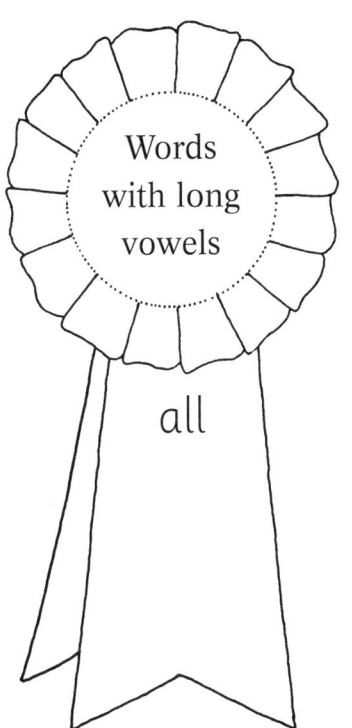

Words with short vowels — full

Words with long vowels — all

© Cambridge University Press 1997   Original illustrations by Peter Kavanagh

13 The fixed letter pattern -ight

Main learning objective

For children to recognise the fixed letter pattern -*ight* and to realise that it sounds the same as in words spelt -*ite*.

> **Supporting text**
> *The Pyjama Party*
> June Crebbin
> Text and picture from page 15

Teaching activities

- Write some -*ight* words on the board for children to read aloud (e.g. *light, tight, fight, bright, right, sight, might*). Discuss the vowel quality with the children. Ask them if they can think of any other fixed letter patterns which make the same sound (i.e. -*ite* as in *white, bite, kite*).
- Start two lists on the board, one headed -*ight* and the other -*ite*. Let the children use an alphabet strip to suggest words which rhyme with *light*. Ask them to say which list each word belongs in, and write it down. Which list has more words? (The -*ight* set should be slightly longer.)

The worksheet

- Check that the children understand how to use the word-search box.
- If the children have read *The Pyjama Party*, they could look to check that they have completed the sentences correctly. The sentences should read:

  Jess and Alice were going to sleep the **night** with Emma.
  The children liked the pillow **fight**.
  The **light** from the torches was quite **bright**.
  The children all got a **fright** at the **sight** of the ghost at the window.
  Tom said, "I **might** want to join in."

Reinforcement and extension

- Pairs of children could make a game to reinforce the fixed letter patterns -*ight* and -*ite*:
  1. You need two pieces of A4-size paper, one white and one coloured. Cut each of them into 12 equal pieces.
  2. Write *ight* on eight of the coloured pieces and *ite* on the other four. Write one of the following word beginnings on each of the white pieces: *b, br, f, fr, k, l, n, qu, r, s, t, wh*.
  3. Place all the pieces face down on a table.
  4. The children take it in turns to turn up two pieces, one white and one coloured. If the two pieces together make a word, and the child can read it aloud, they keep those pieces. If not, they replace them on the table.
  5. When all the letters have been claimed, the child with the most words is the winner.

Words ending in -ight

13 Name _____ Date _____

Two at a time, everyone had a pillow f**ight**.

In each line across there is a word ending in -ight.
Find the words and write them in the torches.

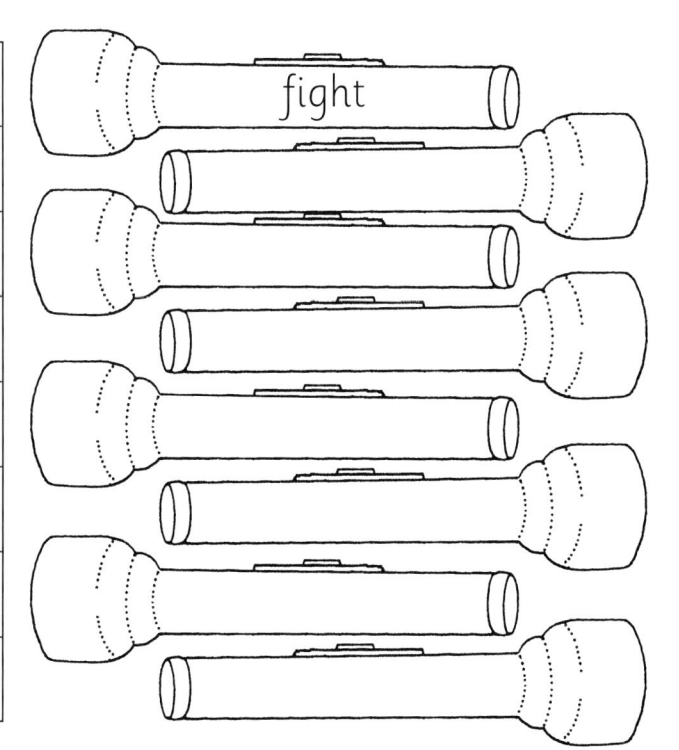

i	g	t	f	i	g	h	t
f	r	i	g	h	t	i	g
r	t	g	l	i	g	h	t
i	g	h	n	i	g	h	t
g	h	m	i	g	h	t	g
h	t	b	r	i	g	h	t
r	i	g	h	t	g	h	t
g	s	i	g	h	t	i	g

fight

Write one of the words you found in each gap.

Jess and Alice were going to sleep the _____ with Emma.

The children liked the pillow _____ .

The _____ from the torches was quite _____ .

The children all got a _____ at the _____ of the ghost at the window.

Tom said, "I _____ want to join in."

© Cambridge University Press 1997   Original illustrations by Peter Kavanagh

14 Stressed and unstressed syllables

Main learning objective

For children to recognise, aurally, the difference between stressed and unstressed syllables. This is very useful in reading, since vowels are often affected by stress (e.g. contrast the -a- in *princi**pal*** and ***pal**ace*, or the -y in *happy* and *supply*).

> **Supporting text**
> *Nonsense*
> *Edited by Richard Brown and Kate Ruttle*
> Poems from pages 14, 20 and 22

Teaching activities

- Choose a child with a name which has two (or more) syllables, write the name on the board and ask the children to read it aloud. Draw a line under the stressed syllable in a different colour (e.g. E*liz*abeth, *Vik*ash, *An*ya, *Thom*as, Vic*to*ria), and introduce the children to the term 'stressed syllable'. Repeat with more names.
- Encourage the children to play with the stress in a familiar word by moving it to different syllables (e.g. *croc*odile, cro*co*dile, croco*dile*).
- Write a selection of words on the board based on a particular theme (e.g. *wolf, monkey, baboon, hyena, elephant, rhinoceros, hippopotamus, caterpillar*). Read them one by one with the children and decide where the stress falls. Then clap out the syllables of one of the words without saying which one it is, emphasising the stress by saying 'di-DUM-di-di' (etc.) as you clap. Ask the children which of the words it is. Continue with other words from the list.
- Choose a poem or rhyme that the children know and ask them to chant it with you. As you chant it for the second time, clap on the stressed syllables. On the third time through, ask the children to join in with clapping the stressed syllables (children tend to find this surprisingly easy).
- Write out some simple poems and show them to the children (e.g. on an overhead projector). Ask one child to underline the stressed syllables while the rest of the class chant and clap the rhyme.

The worksheet

- The children could work in pairs to complete the worksheet activity, one reading and clapping the poems as the other underlines (as described above).
- Note that there are several possible variations in the stress patterns in the second and third poems, so you should accept any reasonable stress marking as long as the children can read the poem aloud using the stress that they have marked.

Reinforcement and extension

- Draw the children's attention to the stress pattern in the first two poems on the worksheet ('di DUM di DUM di DUM di DUM' and 'DUM di di DUM di'). The children could read some more simple poems with strong stress patterns. On a second reading, the group could chant the poem aloud, clapping on the stressed syllables.

Stressed and unstressed syllables

14 Name _____ Date _____

Read these three poems aloud.
Underline the stressed syllables in each poem.

As <u>I</u> was <u>go</u>ing <u>up</u> the <u>stair</u>
I <u>met</u> a man who wasn't there.
He wasn't there again today –
Oh, how I wish he'd go away.

<u>Li</u>ttle Miss Muffet
Sat on a tuffet
Eating her Irish stew.
Along came a spider
Who sat down beside her
And so she ate him up too.

For a lark,
For a prank,
Old Hank
Walked a plank.
These bubbles mark

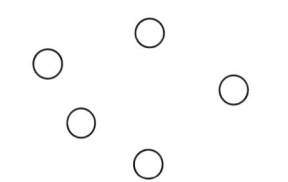

Where Hank sank.

© Cambridge University Press 1997   Original illustrations by Martin Chatterton

15 Words ending in consonant + *le*

Main learning objective

For children to recognise the fixed letter pattern 'consonant + *le*' at the end of words of more than one syllable. Its pronunciation is not as obvious to children as vowel + *l* in words such as *chapel*, *squirrel*, *symbol*, *nostril* and *special* where the pronunciation of vowel and -*l* in the final syllable is mirrored by the spelling. Children also need to recognise that the -*e* in the -*le* fixed letter pattern is not magic -*e*. They need to realise the importance of looking at the whole word before they begin to sound it out.

> **Supporting text**
> *The Slippery Planet*
> Rosemary Hayes
> Picture and text from page 14

Teaching activities

- Re-read a book with the children, listing any two-syllable words which end in a consonant + *le* (e.g. *able*, *apple*, *bottle*, *chuckle*, *giggle*, *gobble*, *little*, *middle*, *paddle*, *pebble*, *people*, *puddle*, *struggle*, *table*, *trouble*, *turtle*, *whistle*).
- Ask the children to read the words in the completed list aloud, listening to the stress pattern. They should observe that all the words have the pattern 'DUM-di' (e.g. *little*), as the consonant + *le* fixed letter pattern is always unstressed.
- Ask the children to pick out from the list all the words where there is a doubled consonant before -*le* (e.g. *apple*, *bottle*, *giggle*, *middle*). What do they notice about the vowel before the doubled consonant? (It is always short.) If you have examples with -*ck*- before -*le*, point out that the vowel here is also short (they have already learnt on worksheet 6 that vowels are short before the fixed letter pattern -*ck*).
- The activity on the worksheet should reinforce the skill of 'chunking' words using fixed letter patterns (see Introduction, page 7). It should alert children to the importance of looking at the pattern of the whole word before trying to sound out individual parts of it. Focus the children's attention on the word beginnings *li*- and *cra*- on the left-hand side, and ask them if they know whether to pronounce them with a long or short vowel sound. Make sure they can see that there is no way of knowing which pronunciation is correct until you look at the ending with which the letters will match. Demonstrate that if you changed the -*ckle* ending to -*dle*, then the *cra*- vowel would change from short to long.

The worksheet

- The words on the worksheet are: *horrible*, *little*, *struggle*, *terrible*, *people*, *impossible*, *crackle* and *trouble*.

Reinforcement and extension

- The children could make up their own version of the matching activity on the worksheet for their friends to do, using different words. (They could use ones from the list you made earlier or search for new ones in another book they have read.) The process of deciding where to divide the words will further reinforce the skill of 'chunking' the words into recognisable bits. It is important that the worksheet that the children make for their friends ends with the instruction to write out the whole word.

Words ending in -le

15 Name _____ Date _____

Suddenly, the boys were struggling inside a net! And all round them were the horri**ble** bright green peo**ple**.

Join these word beginnings and word endings to make proper words.

horri - - - - - - - - - - - - - - ggle
                                              - - ble
li

stru   ttle

terri   ple

peo   ble

impossi   ble

cra   ble

trou   ckle

Write the words you made. Read them aloud.

16 Vowel + *r* in monosyllables

Main learning objective

For children to recognise the fixed letter patterns *-ar, -er, -ir, -or, -ur* in words with one syllable.

> **Supporting text**
> *Coyote Girl*
> Rosalind Kerven
> Picture and text from page 4

Teaching activities

- Use these activities in conjunction with teacher's page 17, which deals with the fixed letter patterns *-are, -ere, -ire, -ore, -ure*. (Note that vowel + *rr* in *two*-syllable words, and *-er* at the end of words, will be dealt with in teacher's pages 18 and 28.)
- Re-read a book with which the children are already familiar, focusing on words of one syllable which feature a vowel + *r*. List the words as you encounter them.
- When you have completed the list, cross out any words where the *r* is followed by *e* (e.g. *care, fire*). (Tell the children that you will talk about these words another time.) Ask the children to read out all the remaining words and to tell you how each of the fixed letter patterns is pronounced. In many accents, *-er, -ir* and *-ur* are pronounced in the same way (so that *fir* and *fur* are homophones).

Note: Some regional variations in accent may be highlighted during the activities on this page and the following page (vowel + *re*). Many Scots, West Country, Lancashire and North American speakers, for example, will pronounce the /r/ after the vowel. Share any of these pronunciation differences with the class to enhance their appreciation of accents.

The worksheet

- Check that the children find all the vowel + *r* words on the worksheet – they often occur in small grammatical words and are easy to overlook. They should then work in pairs to sort the words, with one child reading each word aloud while the other decides on the right cup.
- At the end, they should both read all the words in the cups aloud again before saying how each letter pattern is pronounced.

Reinforcement and extension

- The children could make a worksheet of their own, based on this one but using a different book. They should avoid vowel + *re* spelling patterns.
- Ask the children if they can think of any words which contain the fixed letter patterns on the worksheet but in which they are pronounced differently. If they cannot think of any, help them by suggesting they consider words beginning with *w*. (The obvious examples are words with the *wa-* fixed letter pattern such as *warm*, which the children should remember from worksheet 11, but they may also suggest *word, work* and *worm*.)

Vowel + r in one-syllable words

16 Name _____ Date _____

That Blue **Cor**n Maiden is no friend of mine. I don't even care if I h**ur**t h**er**.

Circle all the words which have a vowel + r.

Blue Corn Maiden was forced to go outside.

It hit her in the chest so hard that she tumbled to the ground.

When she woke up, it was almost dark.

Nothing hurt, but she found that she had thick, grey-brown fur.

The first man agreed.

She sent some people to show the girl her way.

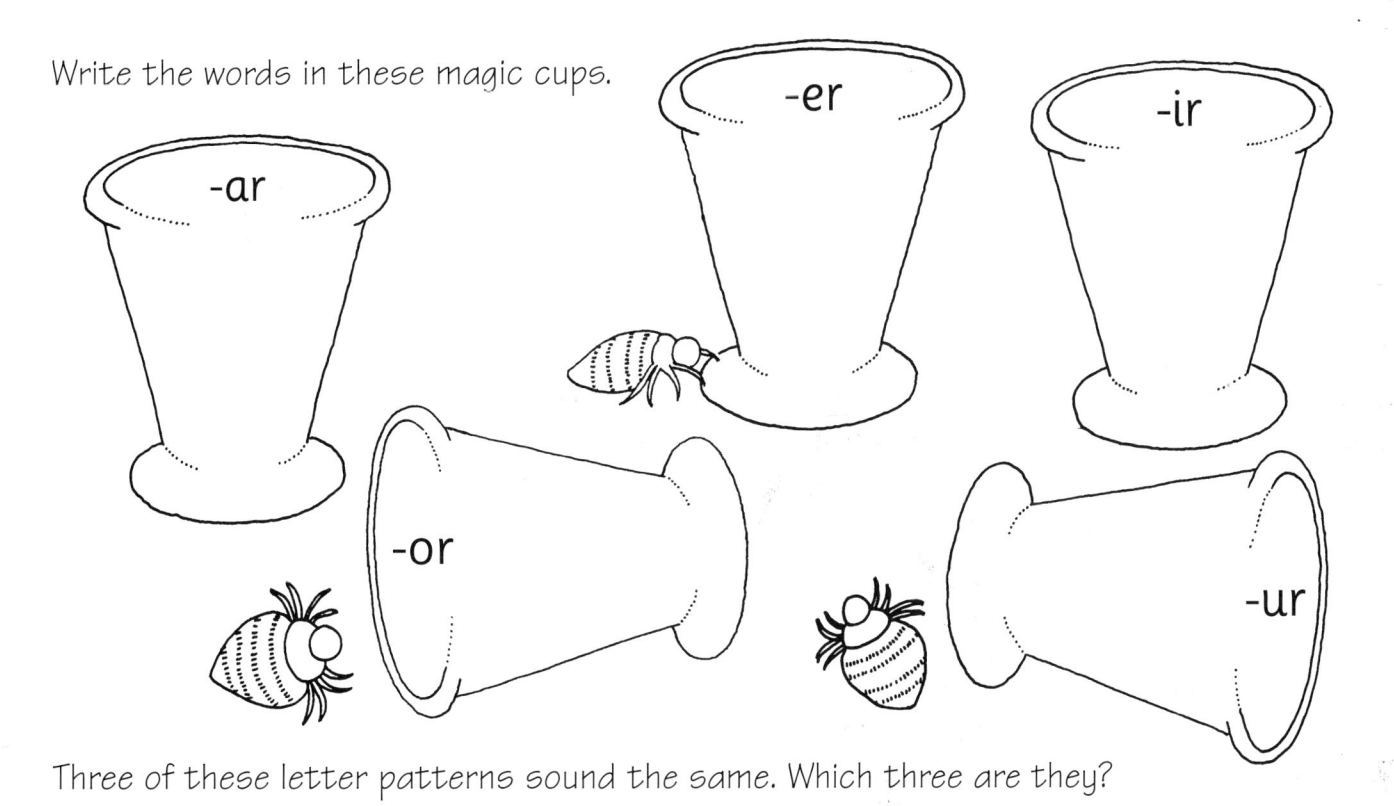

Write the words in these magic cups.

-ar   -er   -ir   -or   -ur

Three of these letter patterns sound the same. Which three are they?

© Cambridge University Press 1997   Original illustrations by Amanda Hall

17 Vowel + *re* in monosyllables

Main learning objective

To familiarise children with the pronunciation of fixed letter patterns involving a vowel + *re*. This pattern frequently occurs at the end of words, or followed by suffixes such as *-ful* or *-less* (e.g. *careful, careless*).

> **Supporting text**
> *The Haystack*
> Richard Brown
> Picture and text from page 21

Teaching activities

- The children should have completed the activities on teacher's page 16 before undertaking these activities.
- Make a list of pairs of words with vowel + *r* and vowel + *re* (e.g. *car/care, her/here, fir/fire, or/more, purr/pure*). Ask the children to read each pair of words, and discuss with them how the vowel sounds differ in each word. In many accents *-or* and *-ore* are pronounced in the same way, and, whereas *-er*, *-ir* and *-ur* all sound the same, *-ere*, *-ire* and *-ure* all differ.
- Ask the children to suggest more words which share each of the vowel + *re* patterns (e.g. *are, care, dare, glare, share, stare; here, there, where, were; hire, fire, wire; core, more, snore, shore, store; cure, pure, sure*). Read all the words aloud with the children, and ask them in which groups all the words sound the same (*-ire*, *-ore* and *-ure*; in *-are* there is one exception, the word '*are*' itself). Point out that there are three different sounds in the *-ere* group (as in *there, were* and *here*).
- Ask the children to complete the first part of the worksheet (finding words on matchsticks), encouraging them to look for the vowel + *re* fixed letter patterns in order to determine word boundaries.
- Point out to the children that this is another case where it is essential to look at the whole word before sounding out its parts, to see whether a vowel + *r* is followed by *-e* or not. This obviously affects its pronunciation. Remind them, too, of the need to listen carefully to what they read – if they pronounce a non-word, they should try an alternative pronunciation.

Reinforcement and extension

- Ask pairs of children to play this game:
  1 Give each pair 10 small pieces of card (about 4 cm × 2 cm). Ask them to write the five vowel + *re* fixed letter patterns (*are, ere, ire, ore, ure*) on five of them, in one colour.
  2 Tell them to write 'word beginnings' onto the remaining five pieces of card in a different colour, chosen from the following: *c, h, sh, st, w, s, b, sc, m, sp*.
  3 They should try to combine the word beginnings with the fixed letter patterns to make as many words as possible, and list these words.
  4 The pair who make the most words are the winners. (With the letters suggested they could make: *care, core, cure; hare, here, hire; share, shire, shore; stare, store; were, wire, wore; sore, sure; bare, bore; scare, score; mare, mere, more; spare, spire, spore.*)

Vowel + re in one-syllable words

17 Name_____ Date_____

It soon fl**are**d up. The trouble was, his **fire** was much too close to the haystack.

Can you find words hidden on the matchsticks? Circle each word.

| f | l | a | r | e | s | t | a | r | e | g | l | a | r | e |

Write the words you found here:
_____

| t | h | e | r | e | f | i | r | e | m | o | r | e | s | u | r | e |

Write the words you found here:
_____

Use some of the words to finish these sentences.

I can't be quite _____ what happened next.

Our mums asked the _____ -fighters to burn our haystack.

We all stood and _____ d as the flames crackled louder and grew bigger.

I raced home for help. There was no-one _____ .

Our mums should have been _____ worried about the height of the haystack.

© Cambridge University Press 1997   Original illustrations by Susan Williams

18 Vowel + *rr* in words with two syllables

Main learning objective

For children to recognise that a double *r* keeps the preceding vowel short in words of two or more syllables.

> **Supporting text**
> ***Coyote Girl***
> Rosalind Kerven
> Picture and text from page 4

Teaching activities

- Ask the children to read the words *hard*, *her*, *girl*, *force* and *hurt* aloud as a reminder of the work they did on vowel + *r* in monosyllables (see teacher's page 16).
- Below these words, write the words *carry*, *merry*, *mirror*, *horror* and *hurry*, and ask the children to read them aloud. What do they notice about the vowel which precedes the *-rr-*? They should observe that the vowel is short in each case, so the lengthening effect of a single *r* does not occur when the *r* is doubled.
- As with worksheet 14, help the children to see how helpful it can be to isolate the initial consonant and then look at a word as vowel + consonant(s) (followed by another vowel + consonant combination in longer words, e.g. *t–err–ible*). If the initial consonant is *w-*, however, this may affect the vowel.

Note: The only common exception to the rule that a vowel is short before *-rr-* is also one of the rare monosyllabic words containing *-rr* – *purr*. It has a long vowel in accents which do not pronounce final /r/.

The worksheet

- The words the children should make on the worksheet are: *horrid*, *arrow*, *quarrel*, *berry*, *sorry*, *hurry*, *carry*, *mirror*. Note that the children will need to use the knowledge they acquired when working on short vowel pronunciation of *wa-* to recognise the word *quarrel*, which is spelt with an *a* but pronounced with /o/ (see teacher's page 10, Reinforcement and extension).

Reinforcement and extension

- Ask the children to copy the beginnings and endings from the worksheet onto small pieces of paper and move them around to see how many other words they can make by combining them. If they are allowed to change the consonants to capital letters as necessary, they may be able to find the following 'extra' words: *barrel*, *curry*, *marry*, *merry*, *quarry*, *Barry*, *Harry*.
- Encourage the children to collect further examples of *-rr-* words from books that they read (e.g. there are several in *Coyote Girl*). Did they find any words of more than two syllables, and does the rule extend to these words, too? (Yes, e.g. *corridor*, *terrible*.)

Vowel + **rr**

18
Name _____ Date _____

"I'll make her **sorr**y for all the bad things she said to me. I'll play a trick on her, that's what I'll do – a really h**orr**id trick."

Make words by joining a beginning and a word ending with a coloured pencil. You can only use each ending once.

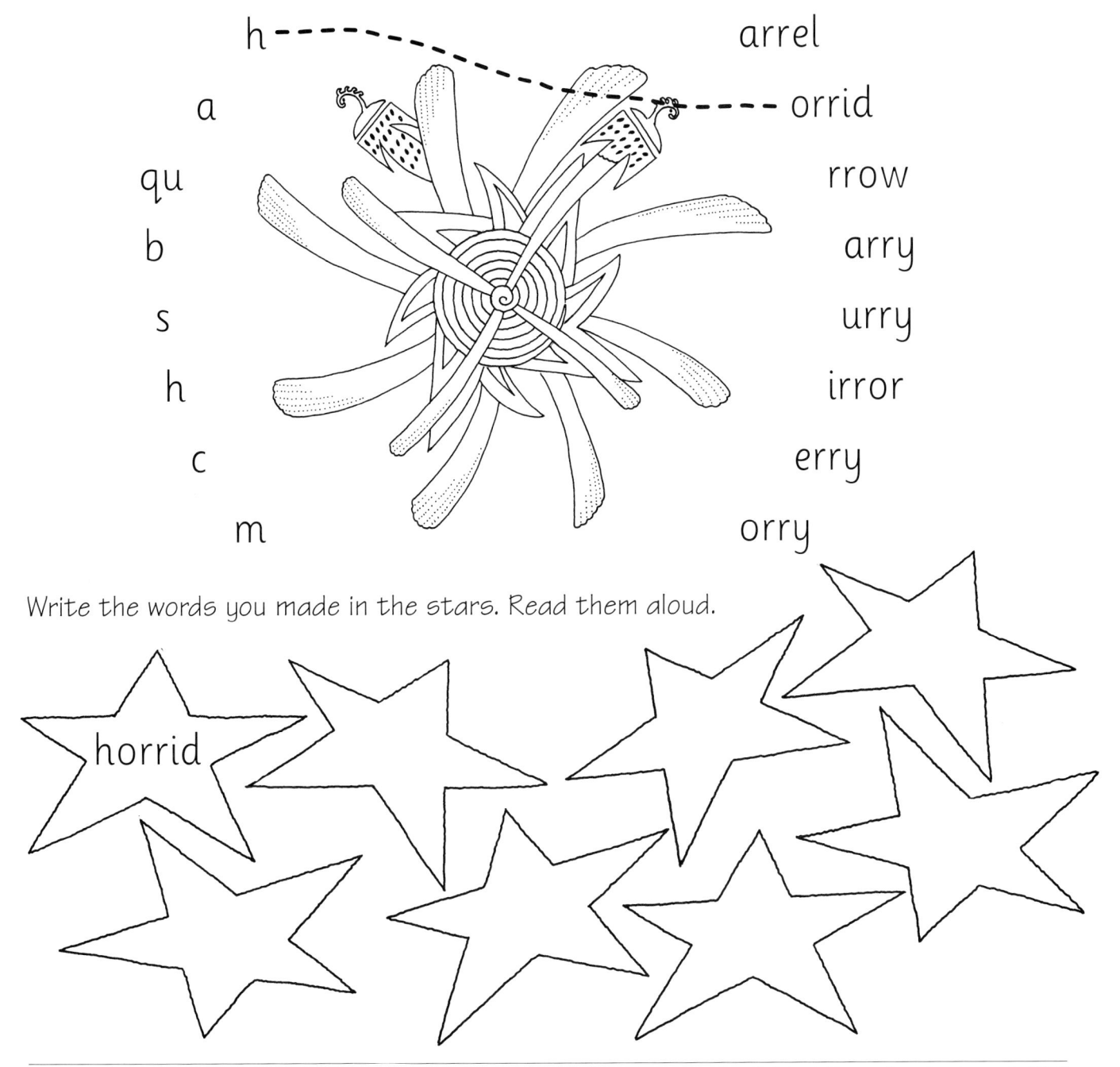

h - - - - - - - - - - - - - - arrel

a   orrid

qu   rrow

b   arry

s   urry

h   irror

c   erry

m   orry

Write the words you made in the stars. Read them aloud.

horrid

© Cambridge University Press 1997   Original illustrations by Amanda Hall

19 Vowel + w

Main learning objective

For children to recognise vowel + *w* as a fixed letter pattern.

> **Supporting text**
> *The Grabbing Bird*
> Rosemary Hayes
> Picture and text from page 5

Teaching activities

- Re-read a book to or with the children (e.g. *The Grabbing Bird*), listing the words which feature vowel + *w* and repeating them aloud as you encounter them.
- Sort the words into sets according to the vowel before the *-w*. Can the children tell you which vowels do not occur in a fixed letter pattern with *-w* (i.e. *i* and *u*)?
- Read the words in each set aloud. The children should notice that the pronunciation of *-aw-* and *-ew-* is consistent whereas *-ow-* can be pronounced as in *clown* or as in *flown*. There is no helpful generalisation as to when each pronunciation is appropriate, so children will have to monitor themselves as they read. (The *clown* pronunciation is slightly more frequent.)

Note: (i) If any children think they have found an example of this fixed letter pattern in the word *away*, explain that fixed letter patterns do not work over syllable boundaries, as in this case. The syllable structure is *a + way*.

(ii) One exception to the normal pronunciation rule for *-ew* is the word *sew*.

The worksheet

- Allow the children to fill in the words in the cloze sentence clues before transferring them to the crossword itself.
- Even if they have read *The Grabbing Bird*, some children may prefer to complete the sentences without looking at the text, in which case they should be encouraged to check their answers in the book afterwards (the relevant page numbers are given after each clue).
- The answers are:
  Across 5 follow, 6 throw, 7 window, 8 flew, 9 glow
  Down 1 yellow, 2 yawning, 3 threw, 4 saw.

Reinforcement and extension

- Ask the children to find other words which include the fixed letter patterns *-aw-*, *-ew-* and *-ow-*. Which one can they find the most examples for?

Vowel + w

19

Name _____ Date _____

The stone started to **glow**. When it stopped **glow**ing, the children **saw** pictures inside it.

Read the clues. You can find the answers inside the grabbing bird. Then fill in the crossword.

Across
5. "Er . . . er . . . _____ us," said the guards. (page 14)
6. As he was about to _____ it away, Sophie stopped him. (page 4)
7. Tom saw a feather flutter past the car _____ . (page 24)
8. All the time, the bird _____ after them. (page 8)
9. The stone became very bright, then it started to _____ . (page 5)

Down
1. It had a huge _____ beak. (page 3)
2. She ran over to warn the guards, but they were _____ so much that they took no notice. (page 17)
3. Then they _____ the stone to the girl. (page 22)
4. They _____ lots of people bouncing up and down. (page 5)

Words in bird: yellow, flew, glow, saw, throw, follow, window, threw, yawning

20 The letter -y in monosyllables

Main learning objective

For children to recognise that, in monosyllabic words, *-y* can act as a vowel, or as a vowel modifier in the fixed letter patterns *-ay*, *-ey*, *-oy* and *-uy*.

> **Supporting text**
> *Snow in the Kitchen*
> Richard Brown
> Picture and text from page 11

Teaching activities

- Write the fixed letter pattern *-ay* on the board and ask the children if they can suggest any words which include it (e.g. *day, play, hay, tray*). Elicit the pronunciation of the fixed letter pattern *-ay*.
- Repeat with the fixed letter patterns *-ey* (e.g. *they, grey*), *-oy* (e.g. *boy, toy, joy*) and *-uy* (e.g. *buy, guy*). Ask the children if there are any with *-iy* (there are none). Point out that *-ay* and *-ey* sound the same.
- Ask the children if they know of any words which do not contain *a, e, i, o* or *u*. If they cannot make any suggestions, write cr-, sk-, tr- and fl- on the board and ask the children to provide the missing letter.
- Discuss the sound which *-y* makes at the end of these words of one syllable. Ask them which of the vowel + *y* letter patterns makes the same sound (*-uy*).

The worksheet

- Point out that some of the word beginnings can be combined with more than one of the fixed letter patterns (e.g. *by, bay, boy, buy*). Encourage them to write down all the possibilities.
- When the children have completed the snowflake activity, ask them to check the spellings in a dictionary. Ensure that the children can read all the words aloud and know their meaning.
- Encourage the children to find examples of these words (and others with these endings), perhaps in their own writing books.

Reinforcement and extension

- The children could make up some more cloze sentences for their friends to fill in.
- If children are confident with *-y* in monosyllabic words, they could work in pairs to find and list longer words ending in *-y* and begin to discuss the pronunciation. (This will be covered in teacher's pages 26 and 27.)

One-syllable words ending in -y

20 Name _____ Date _____

I thought that I'd tr**y** to make that scene with the snow on m**y** tr**ay**.

Add **y**, **ay**, **ey**, **oy** or **uy** to these consonants to make words.

b ____   th ____   m ____

cr ____   pl ____   t ____

sk ____

tr ____   st ____   j ____

Use three of the words to finish these sentences.

Ciss was so sad that she wanted to _____ .

Ciss wanted to _____ in the snow, but she had to _____ inside.

© Cambridge University Press 1997   Original illustrations by Amanda Harvey

21 Verb forms with -ing (1)

Main learning objective

For children to recognise *-ing* as a fixed letter pattern, and for them to identify the base word when they read the *-ing* form. (Verbs ending in magic *-e* will be dealt with on teacher's page 22.)

> **Supporting text**
> ***Cutting and Sticking***
> June Crebbin
> Picture and text from page 4

Teaching activities

- Use these activities in conjunction with (but before) teacher's page 22.
- Play some oral cloze games with the children:
  e.g. I can stick. I'm good at *sticking*.
  I can run. I'm good at _____. etc.
- Write down both forms of some of the verbs you use (e.g. *stick* and *sticking*), avoiding verbs which end in *-e*. Point out the *-ing* fixed letter pattern to the children.
- Write two lists of verbs, one containing verbs to which the *-ing* form can be added without modifying the verb (e.g. *drink, eat, fly, go, sleep, do, feed, feel, hang*) and the other containing verbs which end in a short vowel + consonant (e.g. *begin, chat, clap, grin, shut, hop, let, cut*). Again, avoid those which end in *-e*. Demonstrate to the children how in the first group you just add *-ing* to the verb, whereas with the verbs in the second group you have to double the consonant before adding *-ing*.
- Write a short list of *-ing* forms, some of which have a doubled consonant. Ask the children to read them aloud and tell you what the base word is in each case (i.e. the word without the suffix *-ing*).

Reinforcement and extension

- Ask the children to look through a book they have read, listing examples of *-ing* verbs where the vowel has been doubled.
- Ask them which consonants can be doubled before *-ing*. If they find words such as *hissing* or *sniffing*, do they recognise that the base word already contained a doubled consonant (i.e. *hiss* and *sniff*)?

Words ending in -ing (1)

21 Name _____ Date _____

Alice watched Dad slap**ping** paste onto a piece of wallpaper.
"I can stick," she said. "I'm good at stick**ing**."

Find the words which end in -ing.
Ring the word with a red pencil if the last consonant has been doubled before -ing.
Ring the word with a blue pencil if just -ing has been added.

Jess and Dad were putting up new wallpaper.

Jess was cutting.

"It's not fair, Jess is helping."

She raced around pushing handfuls of newspaper into the bin.

"You're quite good at clearing up."

"How are you getting on?"

Write these words without -ing.

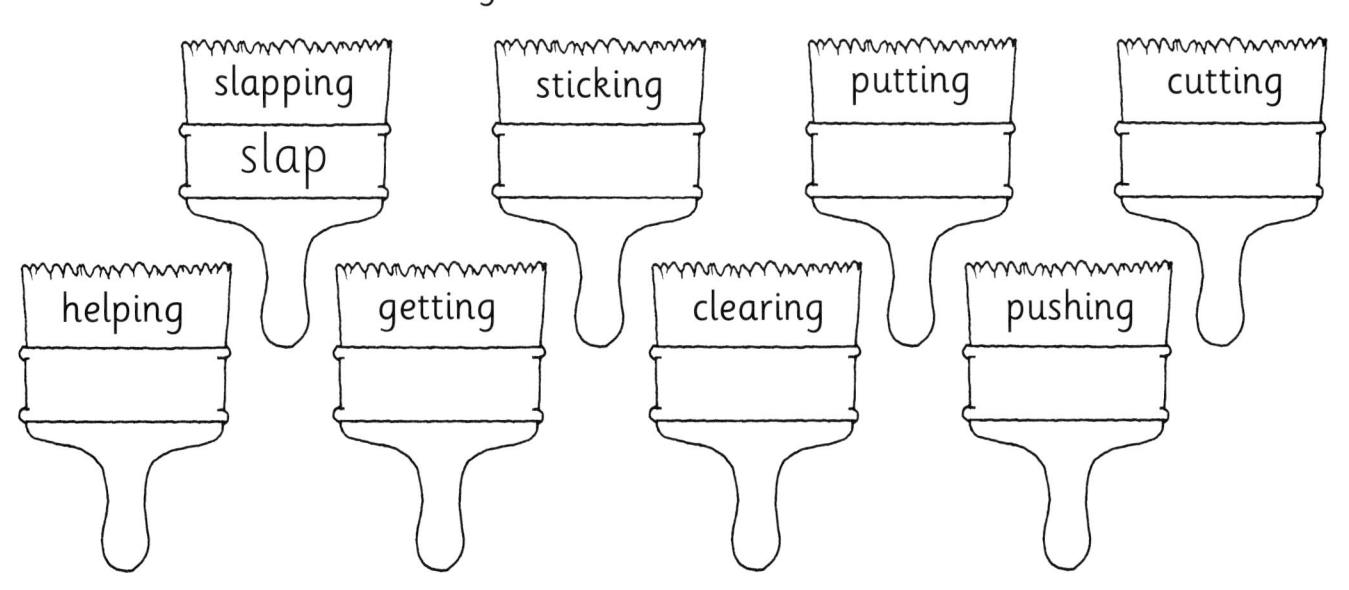

- slapping — slap
- sticking
- putting
- cutting
- helping
- getting
- clearing
- pushing

© Cambridge University Press 1997   Original illustrations by Peter Kavanagh

22 Verb forms with -ing (2)

Main learning objective

For children to recognise that some *-ing* verb forms have a base word ending in magic *-e*. The vowel-changing effect is retained, even though the *-e* is not written.

> **Supporting text**
>
> *The Big Shrink*
> Rosemary Hayes
> Picture and text from page 2

Teaching activities

- The children should have already completed activities from the previous teacher's page before beginning those on this page.
- Write down some verbs which end in a consonant + *e* (e.g. *hope, make, smile, hide, stare, take, write*) and ask the children to read them aloud to remind themselves of the effect of the *-e* (see worksheets 8 and 17).
- Write the equivalent *-ing* form next to each verb, showing the children that the *-e* is lost from the spelling. Ask them to read each *-ing* form aloud so that they can see for themselves that the effect of the *-e* is retained.
- Explain to the children that it is important that, when they read, they can recognise which words have lost the magic *-e* in their spelling. Otherwise they will not know that they have to pronounce the vowel in the base word as a long vowel. It is essential that they look first at the whole word before they start to sound it out from the beginning.
- Re-read a familiar book with the children, picking out verbs with *-ing* as a suffix and deciding with them which ones have had a magic *-e* deleted.
- Give the children some examples of verbs ending in double *e* where the *-e* is not lost when the suffix is added (e.g. *flee → fleeing, agree → agreeing, see → seeing*). Check their understanding of how magic *-e* works by asking them why the *-e* remains in these cases.

Reinforcement and extension

- Blank out the words on the pencil pictures on the worksheet and make photocopies. The children can then make new worksheets for each other by writing *-ing* forms of verbs from a familiar book, or they could choose words connected with a particular theme (e.g. things you do at the seaside – *swimming, splashing, digging, paddling*).
- Children could investigate what happens when you add *-ing* to other base word forms – those ending in *-y* (e.g. *carry, buy*), those ending in a consonant after two vowels (e.g. *meet, shout*) and those ending in *o* (e.g. *go, moo*). They should be able to report back that the base form is not affected.

Words ending in **-ing** (2)

22 Name _____ Date _____

Sam and Jason were star**ing** into their classroom. They couldn't believe their eyes.
A big pen was writ**ing** some words on the board.

Read the word on each pen aloud. Write the words without -ing.

- staring → stare
- buzzing →
- happening →
- writing →
- seeing →
- hoping →
- taking →
- hanging →
- watching →
- going →
- making →

© Cambridge University Press 1997   Original illustrations by Ian Newsham

23 Plural forms

Main learning objective

For children to recognise the fixed letter patterns which mark plural nouns, and for them to be able to identify the base form of a plural noun.

> **Supporting text**
> *The Pyjama Party*
> *June Crebbin*
> Picture and text from page 12

Teaching activities

- Introduce the word 'plural' to children, explaining that it means 'more than one'. Write down some common words which end in one consonant (e.g. *road, cat, colour, window*) and ask the children to tell you the plural form of each. Add the *-s* to each in a colour.
- Write a second list of words which end in *-e* (either magic *-e* as in *cake, kite, line,* or a fixed letter pattern ending in *-e* as in *apple, bottle, table*), avoiding words which end in *-se, -ce, -ge* or *-ze*. Again, ask the children to tell you the plural form, and add the *-s* in a different colour.
- Now make a list of words which are pronounced with a 'hissing' or 'buzzing' consonant sound at the end (e.g. *horse, rose, voice, prize, box, cage, splash, wish, match, peach*). Ask the children to listen hard as they tell you the plurals and tell you how the plural is pronounced – /iz/. Point out that this is spelt *es* (add this to the words in a different colour), but that some of the words already end in *-e*, so only an *-s* is added in those cases.
- Give the children a list of plural forms, including examples of each of the three types covered in the three lists, and ask them to write the singular form. Remind them to look at the pattern of the whole word before deciding whether *-s* or *-es* marks the plural.

Reinforcement and extension

- Give the children a short list of words which end in consonant + *y* (e.g. *pony, cherry, city*). Show them that the plural is formed by adding *-es*, as with the 'hissing' and 'buzzing' words, but that the *-y* also changes to an *-i-*. You could give the children some examples of words ending in *-y* to copy onto the back of the worksheet (e.g. *party* → *parties, teddy* → *teddies, ghost story* → *ghost stories*).
- Ask the children to work in pairs to collect some irregular plurals (e.g. *mouse* → *mice, child* → *children*).
- The children could make a wall chart showing the different regular plural forms as well as some irregular ones.
- Show the children how the *-s* endings on verbs follow a similar pattern to the plural endings (e.g. *add* → *adds, fix* → *fixes, guess* → *guesses, carry* → *carries, fly* → *flies*). Use these words in the context of a sentence, though, so it is clear to the children that these forms do not indicate plural forms as the noun endings did.

Plurals

23
Name _____ Date _____

He drew the curtain**s** so that it was dark. Everyone flashed their torch**es** round and round.

Fill in the missing words.

one _ _ _ _
four faces

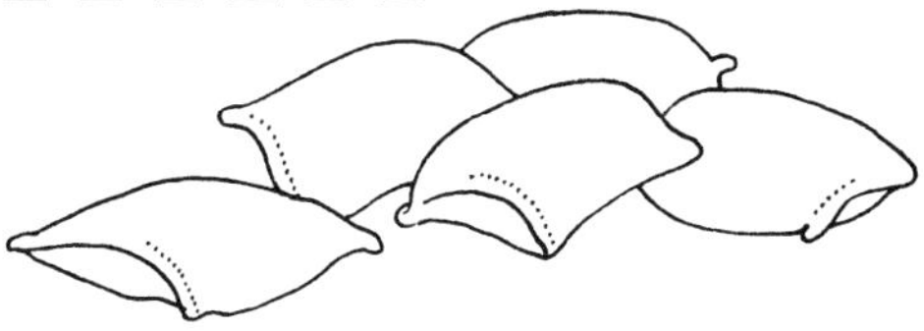

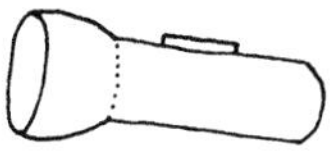

a _ _ _ _ _
two torches

a flower
lots of _ _ _ _ _ _ _ _

a pillow
five _ _ _ _ _ _ _ _

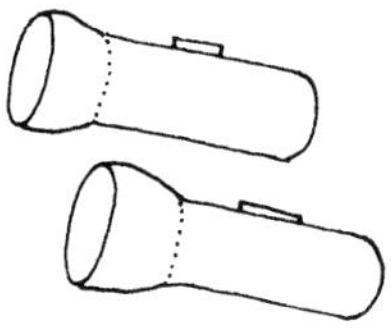

a cat
some _ _ _ _ 

Now think about these:

a ghost
some _____

one jam tart
lots of _____

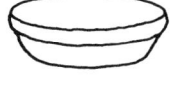

a _____
some games

one dish
two _____

a _____
some girls

24 Verb forms with -ed (1)

Main learning objective

For children to recognise the suffix -*ed* at the end of words, and for them to identify the base word when they read the -*ed* form.

> **Supporting text**
> *The Big Shrink*
> Rosemary Hayes
> Picture and text from page 18

Teaching activities

- Use these activities in conjunction with teacher's page 25, which deals with -*ed* forms of base words which end in -*y*.
- Re-read a book to or with the children (e.g. *The Big Shrink*), listing the words which end in the suffix -*ed*. As you do so, ask the children to read each one, and point out that after a *t* or *d* the -*ed* ending is sounded (pronounced /id/). In all other cases the vowel is not sounded at all.
- Choose words from the list where -*ed* is added to the base form without modification (e.g. *add, ask, call, cheer*). Ask the children what each word would be if the -*ed* ending were removed.
- Move on to words ending in a consonant + *e* where only -*d* is added (e.g. *arrive, bounce, change, dance, hate*). Again, ask the children what the word would be without the ending. (Remind them that some of the verbs end in magic -*e*, and it is important that they recognise this when they look at the -*ed* forms so that they know how to pronounce the vowel.)
- Repeat this with words which end in one vowel and one consonant. Show them that the consonant is doubled before -*ed* is added (e.g. *chat, drag, hop, grin*).

The worksheet

- The cloze passage on the worksheet is taken from *The Big Shrink*, so children who have access to this book could check their answers by looking at pages 10–11. The missing words are: *scuttled, seemed, pulled, squeaked, blinked, rubbed, muttered*.
- Check that the children can read the words on the worksheet aloud, making sure in particular that they do not pronounce the -*ed* as an extra syllable unless it follows *t* or *d*.

Reinforcement and extension

- The children could collect more examples of words ending in the -*ed* suffix and record them on a chart. This should be divided into columns according to how the suffix is added (i.e. 'Add *ed*', 'Double the consonant and add *ed*', 'Add *d*'). After a week, the children should note which column contains the most words.

Words ending in -ed (1)

24 Name _____ Date _____

Sam jump**ed**. He land**ed** on the end of a ruler and it bounc**ed** him into the air. He tumbl**ed** in the air and crash**ed** down beside Jason.

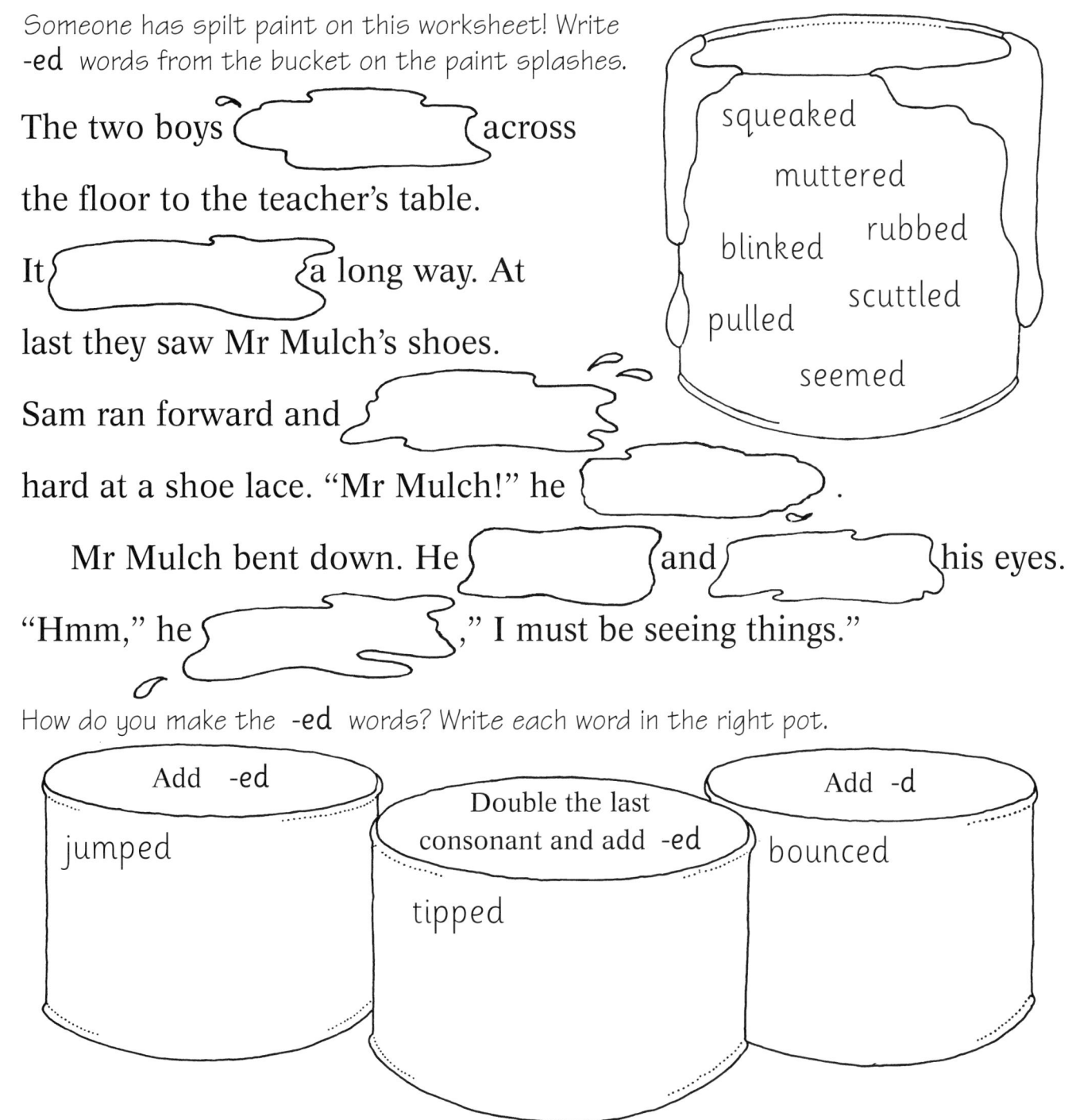

Someone has spilt paint on this worksheet! Write -ed words from the bucket on the paint splashes.

The two boys ⬚ across the floor to the teacher's table. It ⬚ a long way. At last they saw Mr Mulch's shoes. Sam ran forward and ⬚ hard at a shoe lace. "Mr Mulch!" he ⬚.

Mr Mulch bent down. He ⬚ and ⬚ his eyes. "Hmm," he ⬚," I must be seeing things."

Bucket words: squeaked, muttered, blinked, rubbed, pulled, scuttled, seemed

How do you make the -ed words? Write each word in the right pot.

Add -ed	Double the last consonant and add -ed	Add -d
jumped	tipped	bounced

© Cambridge University Press 1997   Original illustrations by Ian Newsham

25 Verb forms with -ed (2)

Main learning objective

For children to recognise that, in base words which end in -y, the -y changes to an -i- before -ed is added.

> **Supporting text**
> *Jumble Power*
> Rosemary Hayes
> Picture and text from page 18

Teaching activities

- The children should have already completed the activities from the previous teacher's page before beginning those on this page.
- Remind the children of how the -ed suffix is added to words. Write a short list of verb forms ending in -ied on the board (e.g. *tried, copied, hurried*) and see if they can work out what the base word is for each word (i.e. *try, copy, hurry*). Write the base word beside each -ied word.
- Ask the children to look at all the base words and tell you how they end. It is important that they observe that the words end in consonant + y (since words which end in a vowel + y retain the y in front of the -ed, e.g. *played, annoyed*).
- Ask the children to read the pairs of words, first the base word and then the -ied form, and tell you how the ending is pronounced. (It is simply a /d/ sound on the end of the base word.)

The worksheet

- When the children complete the worksheet, check that they understand the idea of a machine which changes things in a particular way.

Reinforcement and extension

- Make a word-changing game for the children as follows:
  1. Cut off the top and bottom of four empty breakfast cereal boxes.
  2. Stick a label on each box with a different rule written on it (i.e. 'Add *ed*', 'Add *d*', 'Double the consonant and add *ed*' and 'Change the *y* to an *i* and add *ed*').
  3. Give the boxes to four of the children (or four pairs of children), who should lay them on their sides. Give the other children in the group a marker pen and some slips of paper. Tell the children that the boxes are word-changing machines.
  4. The children with slips of paper should write on each of them a word which they would like the word-changing machines to change (make sure they realise that their words must be verbs). They should then decide which machine to put their word slip through.
  5. If the children 'operating' the machines think that a word is in the right machine, they should 'process' the word in the way described on the label on the machine (i.e. they should write the appropriate -ed form below the verb or on the other side of the slip of paper). If not, they should write REJECT on the slip and return it to the person who put it in.

Note: This game could be adapted, as could the worksheet, for use with plural forms of nouns (see teacher's page 23) or adding the -ing suffix (see teacher's pages 21–22).

Words ending in -ed (2)

25 Name _____ Date _____

The men hurr**ied** back to the table. They took long, bendy metal spoons from their pockets and began to eat.

This is a word-changing machine. As words go through the machine, they obey the instructions on the machine.

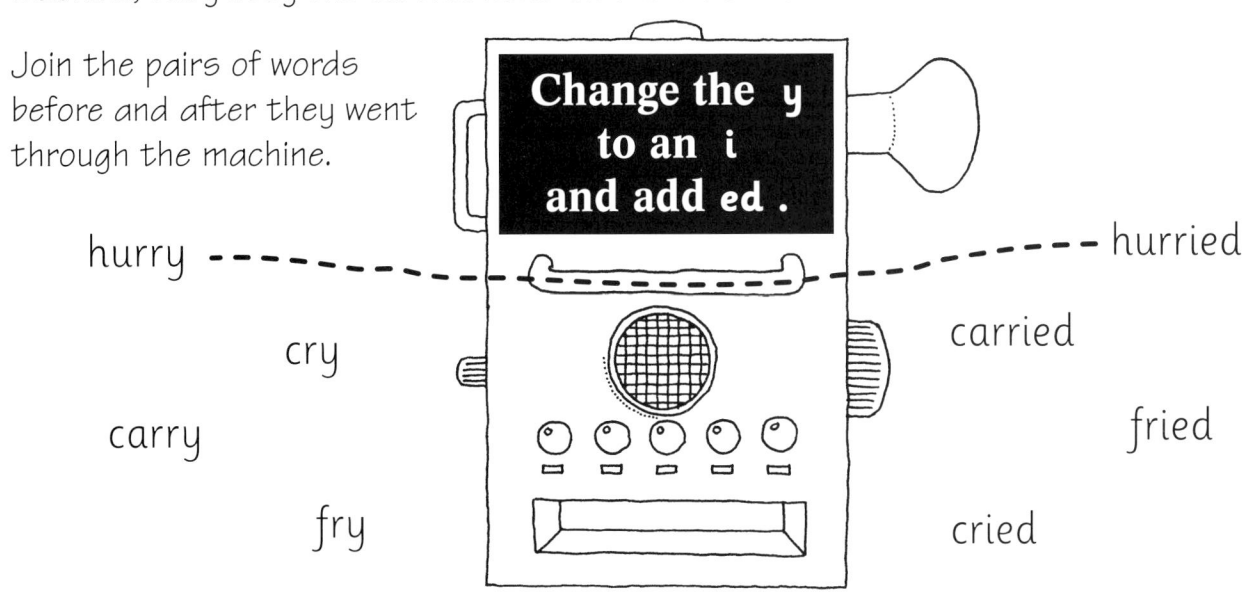

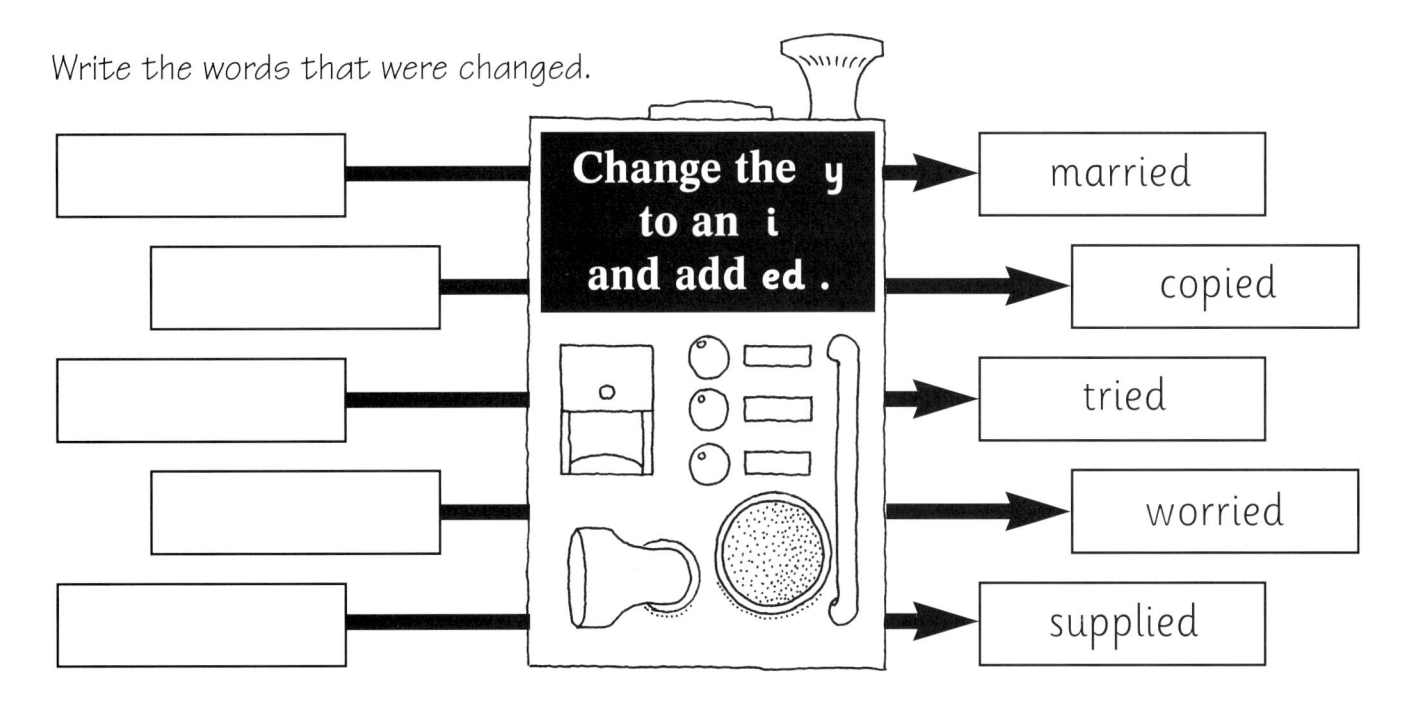

Join the pairs of words before and after they went through the machine.

Change the y to an i and add ed.

hurry - hurried

cry   carried

carry   fried

fry   cried

Write the words that were changed.

Change the y to an i and add ed.

☐ → married
☐ → copied
☐ → tried
☐ → worried
☐ → supplied

© Cambridge University Press 1997   Original illustrations by Ian Newsham

26 Stressed and unstressed syllables in words ending in -y

Main learning objective

For children to understand how the pronunciation of -y is affected by stress.

> **Supporting text**
> *The Magic Sword*
> Rosemary Hayes
> Picture and text from page 3

Teaching activities

- Remind the children of the work they did in worksheet 14 on identifying stressed and unstressed syllables within words. Ask them to clap out what they had for lunch or breakfast, emphasising the stressed syllables (e.g. 'cake and fizzy drinks' – DUM di DUM-di DUM).
- Re-read a book to or with the children (e.g. *The Magic Sword*), listing all the words ending in -y. Read the words aloud with them, emphasising the stress pattern of each word (and clapping it out, if it seems appropriate). Mark the stress pattern by underlining the stressed syllable. (Be aware that some children may pronounce words slightly differently from you or the other children, but equally validly – for instance, the word *really* may be pronounced with two syllables as /riːli/ or with three as /riːəli/. In any case, the variation is not in the stressed syllable but in the number of unstressed syllables.)
- Sort the words into two sets according to whether the -y is in a stressed or unstressed syllable.
- Read through the words in the sets and ask the children to listen carefully to the way in which the -y is pronounced at the end of each word. They should notice that in unstressed syllables the -y makes a short /i/ sound (e.g. *lady, every*) but that in stressed syllables the -y is pronounced as a long vowel sound (e.g. *supply, cry, annoy*).

Reinforcement and extension

- The children could search for words ending in -y in another book, sorting them into sets as described above. Which set contains the most words?
- Ask the children to look for examples of words which have -y- in the middle of the word (e.g. *rhyme, rhythm, Egypt, cycle, tyre, type, mystery, sympathy*). They should consider the sound made by -y- in each of these words.
- If the children already know about different parts of speech, they could divide a list of words ending with -y into nouns, verbs, adjectives and adverbs. Can they see any patterns emerging? (Teacher's page 27 develops this further.)

Stressed and unstressed -y

26 Name _____ Date _____

'Where's your teacher?" asked Karen's mum.
"She's aw**ay**," said Karen.
We've got a suppl**y** teacher tod**ay**."

Read aloud all these words ending in y. Use a coloured pencil to underline the stressed syllable.

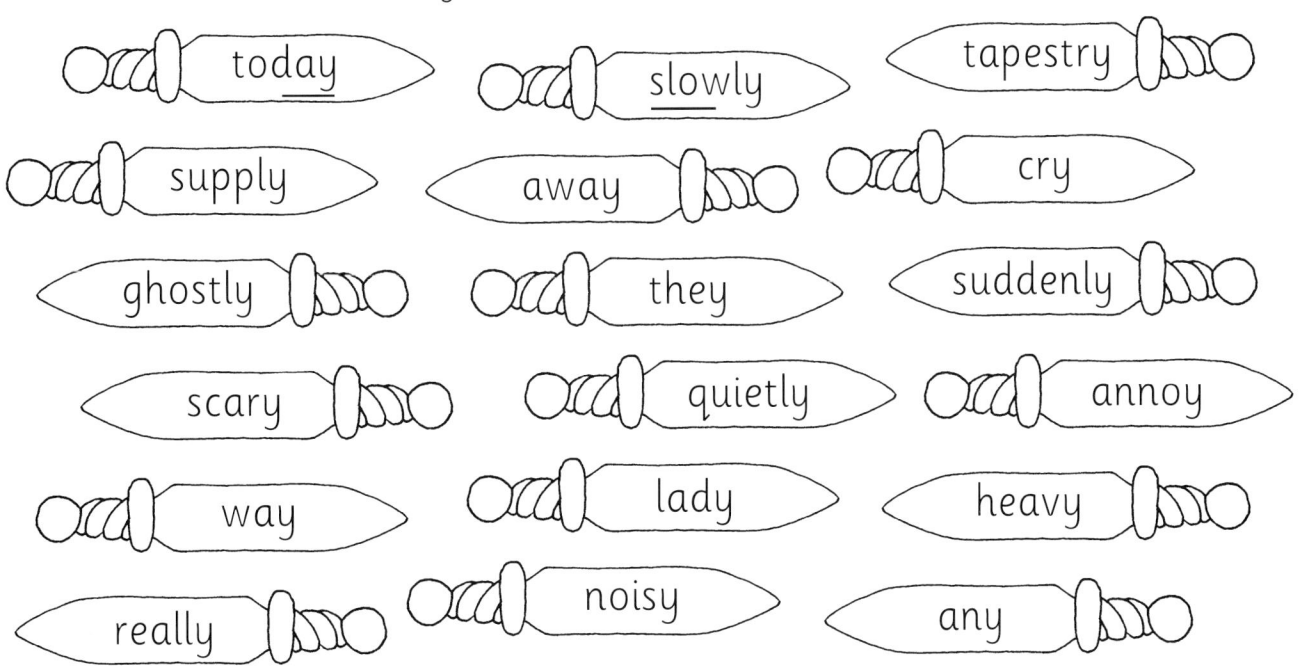

- tod<u>ay</u>
- <u>slow</u>ly
- tapestry
- supply
- away
- cry
- ghostly
- they
- suddenly
- scary
- quietly
- annoy
- way
- lady
- heavy
- really
- noisy
- any

Write the words on the right shield.

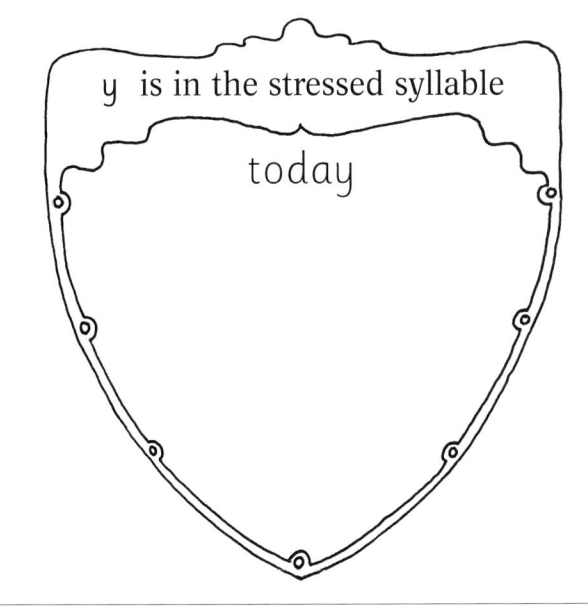

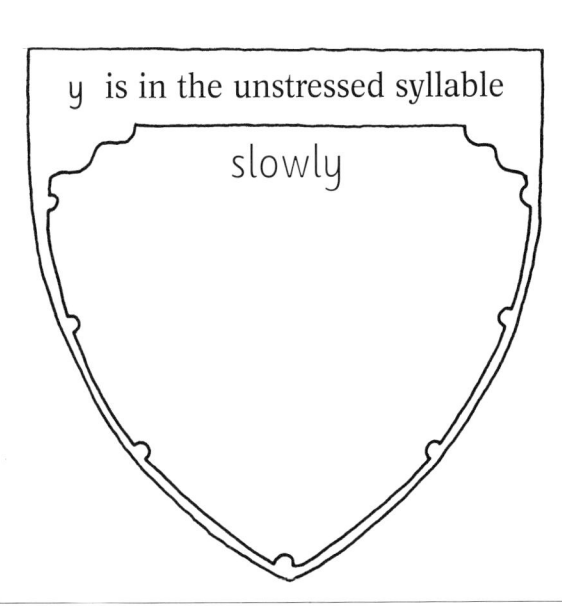

y is in the stressed syllable
today

y is in the unstressed syllable
slowly

27 The suffixes -y and -ly for adjectives and adverbs

Main learning objective

For children to recognise the base word when they meet adjectives ending in -y or adverbs ending in -ly.

> **Supporting text**
> *The Grabbing Bird*
> Rosemary Hayes
> Picture and text from page 14

Teaching activities

- Re-read a book to or with the children (e.g. *The Grabbing Bird*), listing the 'describing' words which end in -y or -ly.
- Ask the children to divide the words in the list into two sets: one of adjectives (i.e. words which describe a noun) and the other of adverbs (i.e. words which describe how an action is done).
- Ask them if they can see any pattern to the word endings in the two groups. They should be able to tell you that the adjectives end in -y and the adverbs in -ly.
- Ask the children to tell you what the base word is for each of the adjectives and adverbs. Write the base word beside each adjective and adverb, indicating in another colour the letters that have been added or removed, as follows:

sudden sudden + LY	luck luck + Y
tight tight + LY	fun fun + n + Y
immediate immediate + LY	wav(e) wav + Y
eas(y) eas + i + LY	trembl(e) trembl + Y
gentl(e) gentl + Y	ang(e)r angr + Y

- Point out to the children that, if a magic -e is taken away before -y, the effect of the magic -e on the preceding vowel still remains (e.g. in *wavy*).
- It is important to remind children to listen to themselves as they read, to check that they have not read nonsense. For instance, if a child reads the word *slimy* as 'slimmy', they should pause and reconsider. Recognising that *slimy* is related to *slime* should help them self-correct accurately.

The worksheet

- The answers to the worksheet crossword are:
  Across 6 anxiously, 7 sleepy, 8 carefully, 9 suddenly;
  Down 1 trembly, 2 slowly, 3 tightly, 4 wavy, 5 bouncy.

Reinforcement and extension

- Give each pair of children ten small pieces of paper and ask them to write on each one either an adjective ending in -y or an adverb ending in -ly. The children should then swap their pile of words with another pair of children. They should try to write sentences using each of the adjectives and adverbs in their new pile.
- Give the children some short cloze sentences, missing out adjectives and adverbs (e.g. *The _____ giant ran _____ to the _____ castle*). The children should suggest different ways to fill each gap, such as the following:

happy	**quickly**	**gloomy**
The **healthy** giant ran **stealthily** to the **stony** castle.
hungry	**noisily**	**lovely**
	painfully	

27 'Describing' words ending in -y or -ly

Name _____ Date _____

"We've brought the stone," gasped Sophie, looking anxious**ly** over her shoulder.

Read the clues. You can find the answers in the bouncy castle. Then fill in the crossword.

Words in castle: suddenly, tightly, carefully, trembly, anxiously, bouncy, slowly, sleepy, wavy

Across
6. "We've brought the stone," gasped Sophie, looking _____ over her shoulder.
7. The three guards were very fat and _____ .
8. Tom placed the stone _____ in the case.
9. _____ Sophie stopped and grabbed Tom's arm.

Down
1. "What are you doing here?" she asked in a high, _____ voice.
2. Very _____ they bounced off down a passageway.
3. The bird tried to grab the stone, but Tom held on _____ .
4. A girl with _____ hair bounced up.
5. "We must take it back to the _____ castle."

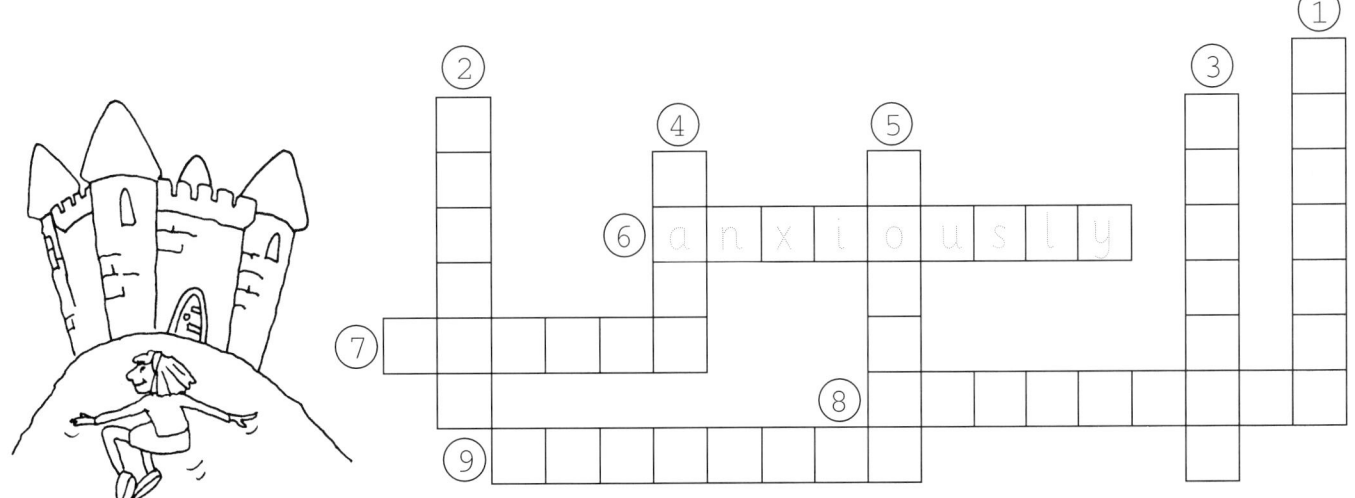

6 across: anxiously

© Cambridge University Press 1997   Original illustrations by Ian Newsham

28 Unstressed -er (-ar, -or, -re) as a final syllable

Main learning objective

For children to recognise that there are a variety of fixed letter patterns at the end of words which make the same sound as the last syllable of *bigger* (i.e. /ə/ or /ər/, depending on whether they speak an /r/pronouncing accent). The worksheet focuses on the endings *-er, -ar, -or* and *-re*.

> **Supporting text**
>
> *A Cat for Keeps*
> June Crebbin
> Picture and text from page 30

Teaching activities

- Give the children some examples (orally) of names which end in /ə/ (e.g. *Peter, Jamila, Christopher, Hannah, Sara, Carla*). Ask the children if any of their names or the names of their friends end in this sound, and if so, ask them to write these names on the board. (Note that this activity will not work if there are children in the group who pronounce /r/ at the end of words – for them, *Peter* will not have the same ending as *Jamila*! Check for /r/ pronouncers by asking whether *Sita* rhymes with *Peter*, or *Hannah* with *banner*.)
- Underline the endings of the names. Point out that, despite the different spellings, all these endings sound the same.
- Divide the children into pairs. Give each pair a different book (one with which they are familiar). Ask them how many words they can find with each of the endings *-er, -ar, -or* and *-re* (as a final unstressed syllable) in ten minutes. The children should then read their words aloud to the other pairs. Ask them to count the number of words with each ending – which ending yielded the most examples?

The worksheet

The answers to the crossword on the worksheet are:

Across 3 letter, 5 whiskers, 6 actor, 7 after, 8 other, 9 never;
Down   1 flowers, 2 collar, 4 theatre.

Reinforcement and extension

- Discuss how the letter patterns *-er, -ar, -or* and *-re* are pronounced in *stressed* syllables (e.g. *flower/her, collar/farm, actor/form, theatre/care*). (See also worksheet 17.)
- Ask the children why it is therefore important to look at the pattern of the whole words before attempting to sound them out (i.e. because the pronunciation of these letter strings is affected by whether or not they are stressed).
- Ask the children if they can find any other word endings which make the same sound (/ə/) as in *bigger* (e.g. *-a* as in *coca-cola* and *Emma*, *-ure* as in *creature* and *future*, *-our* as in *colour* and *flavour*). Ask the children to find other words with these endings, and list them on a wall chart. Which one can they find the most examples for?
- The children could make up their own crosswords for their friends, using words with as many different unstressed endings as possible.

Unstressed -er, -ar, -or and -re

28 Name _____ Date _____

'Trust one stray kitten to find another," said Mum.

Read the words in the cat aloud. Listen to the last vowel sound in each word.
Use the words to do the crossword.

Words in the cat: collar, flowers, other, letter, whiskers, theatre, never, after, actor

Across
3. Tom got a _____ from Uncle Jack.
5. Tom saw a big brown cat with white _____ .
6. Uncle Jack was an _____ .
7. _____ the interval, everyone sang a song.
8. People were bumping into each _____ .
9. " _____ go off like that again", said Dad.

Down
1. The actors each got a bunch of _____ .
2. Lucky the cat wore a red _____ .
4. The pantomime was in a _____ .

29 Common prefixes (*a-*, *be-*, *re-*, *un-*)

Main learning objective

For children to recognise some of the more common prefixes and to understand that they are usually unstressed.

> **Supporting text**
> *A Shoot of Corn*
> *Richard Brown*
> Picture and text from page 7

Teaching activities

- Write lists of words on the board which feature common prefixes such as the following:
    - ***a-*** *(about, above, across, afloat, ahead, amuse, amaze, among)*
    - ***be-*** *(become, because, before, bedraggled, begin, behind, believe, below)*
    - ***re-*** *(reflect, refuse, relieved, remember, remind, remain, remove, repeat)*
    - ***un-*** *(uncurl, uneasy, ungrateful, unless, unscrew, unusual, unable)*

- Read aloud from the words on the list, emphasising the stressed second syllable. Tell the children that these words all begin with 'prefixes'. Explain that prefixes are a special set of fixed letter patterns which always occur at the beginning of words and which are usually unstressed (e.g. *unusual, dishonest, pretend*).

- Read the words aloud again, asking the children to concentrate on the pronunciation of the vowel in the prefix. Point out that the pronunciation of unstressed vowels in the first syllable of a word is not necessarily the same as in the final syllable of a word (e.g. listen to each *e* in *remember* – the first *e* (unstressed) makes the sound /i/, the second (stressed) /e/ and the last (unstressed) /ə/).

- Explain to the children that it is helpful for them to recognise some common prefixes because in words with two syllables it can be a problem deciding which to stress. If they read a word and it does not make sense, they should check whether it begins with one of these prefixes and try moving the stress to the second syllable.

The worksheet

- The words that could be made include:
  behind   afraid   until   believed/relieved
  unlikely   around   unusual
  unkind   recover/uncover   return   became

Reinforcement and extension

- Give the children some more common prefixes and ask them to find example words for them:
    - ***dis-*** (e.g. *disappear, disappoint, discover, disgust, display*)
    - ***de-*** (e.g. *decide, delicious, delight*)
    - ***ex-*** (e.g. *except, excite, expect, expensive*)
    - ***to-*** (e.g. *tomorrow, together, tonight, towards*)
    - ***pre-*** (e.g. *prefer, predict, prevent*)

- Put up a 'prefixes' chart on the wall and invite children to write on it any word they find which they think has a prefix. The clue to their discovery is to think of lots of words which begin with the same unstressed syllable.

- You could make a set of dominoes from thin cardboard for children to practise making words with prefixes. On the right-hand half of each domino you should write a common prefix. On the left-hand half, in a different colour, you should write an 'ending' with which one of the prefixes can match to make a word. The children should follow the rules for a standard game of dominoes.

Prefixes

29   Name _____   Date _____

I **re**member one harvest festival in particular. I was **a**bout eight.

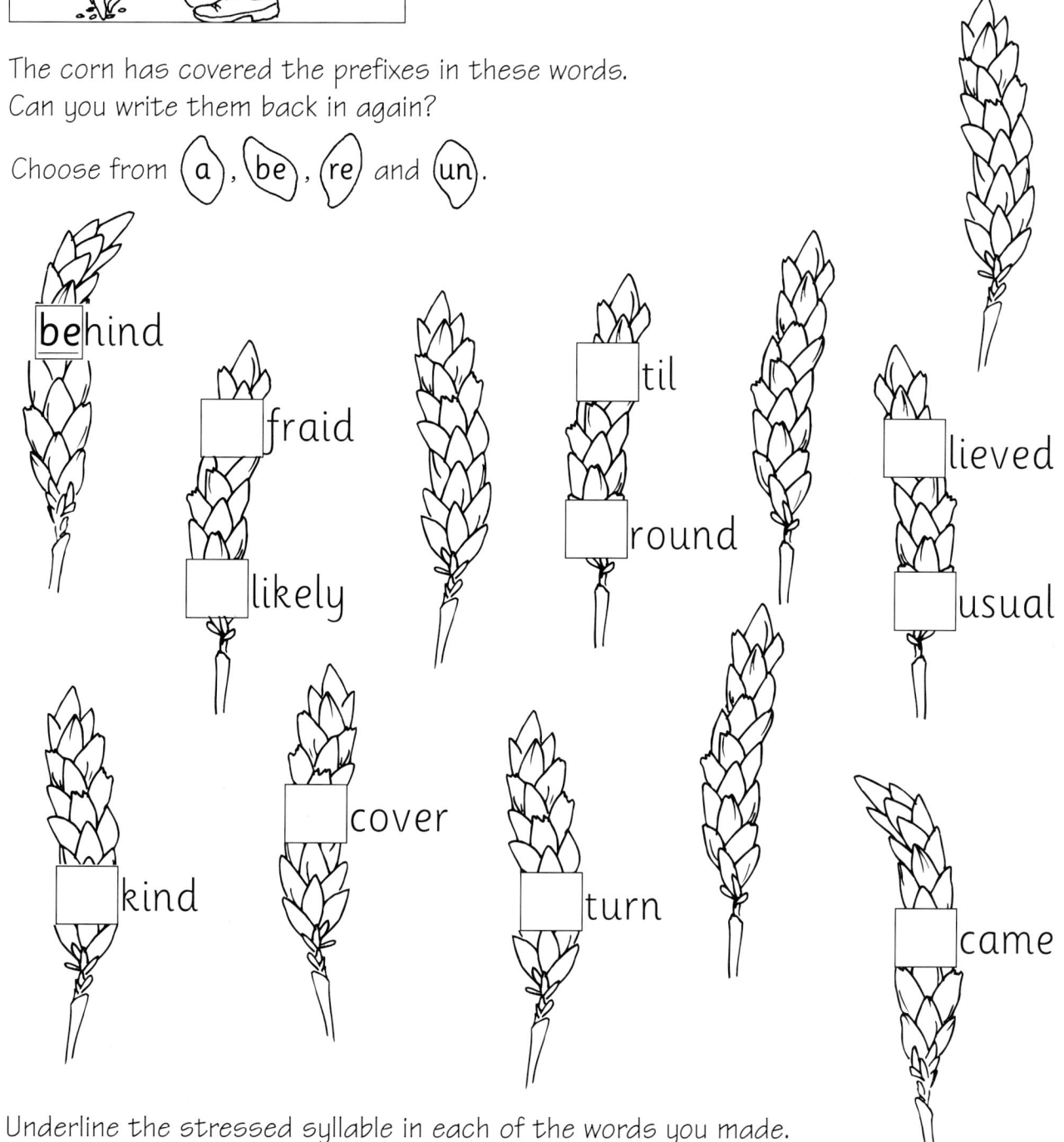

The corn has covered the prefixes in these words.
Can you write them back in again?

Choose from (a), (be), (re) and (un).

[be]hind

[ ]fraid

[ ]likely

[ ]til

[ ]round

[ ]lieved

[ ]usual

[ ]kind

[ ]cover

[ ]turn

[ ]came

Underline the stressed syllable in each of the words you made.

© Cambridge University Press 1997   Original illustrations by Gillian Marklew

30 Compound words (1) – grammatical words

Main learning objective

To familiarise children with common compound words involving grammatical words. They need to learn to identify the 'join' within these words, which is not usually marked with a hyphen.

> **Supporting text**
> *Don't Be Late!*
> June Crebbin
> Picture and text from page 26

Teaching activities

- Write the words *something, everyone* and *anywhere* on the board. Ask the children if they can see words within the words you have written.
- Write the six base words *some, any, every, thing, one,* and *where* on the board, and demonstrate that each of the first three can combine with each of the second three to generate *something, someone, somewhere, anything, anyone, anywhere, everything, everyone* and *everywhere*.
- Read the words aloud and ask one of the children to underline the stressed syllable for each word. In all these words they should underline the first syllable (nearly all compound words have the stress on the first syllable).

The worksheet

- As the children complete the worksheet, remind them of the need to look at the whole word before they assign stress or chunk the word. Recognising compound words is helpful in reading words, but it can lead to difficulties if children do not keep track of the sense of the sentence by constant monitoring. For instance, the word *nowhere* could be quite reasonably chunked and (mis)pronounced as *now-here*, which would not make sense!

Reinforcement and extension

- Ask the children to combine the base words *body, thing, one* and *where* with the word *no*. See if they notice something strange about the pronunciation of one of these words (i.e. *nothing*). Point out that *no-one* is often written with a hyphen (e.g. throughout **Cambridge Reading**) to make its pronunciation clearer.

Something, everyone, anywhere

30 Name _____ Date _____

Then she heard **something**.
She turned round. "Look!" she said.
Everyone turned round.

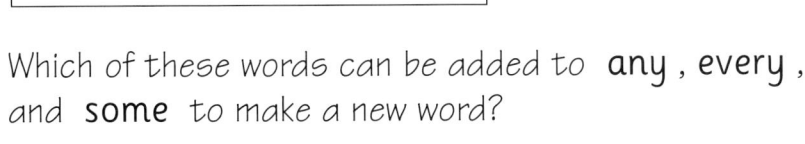

Which of these words can be added to any, every, and some to make a new word?

body   thing   way   times

where   how   what   one

Write the words you make in these fields.

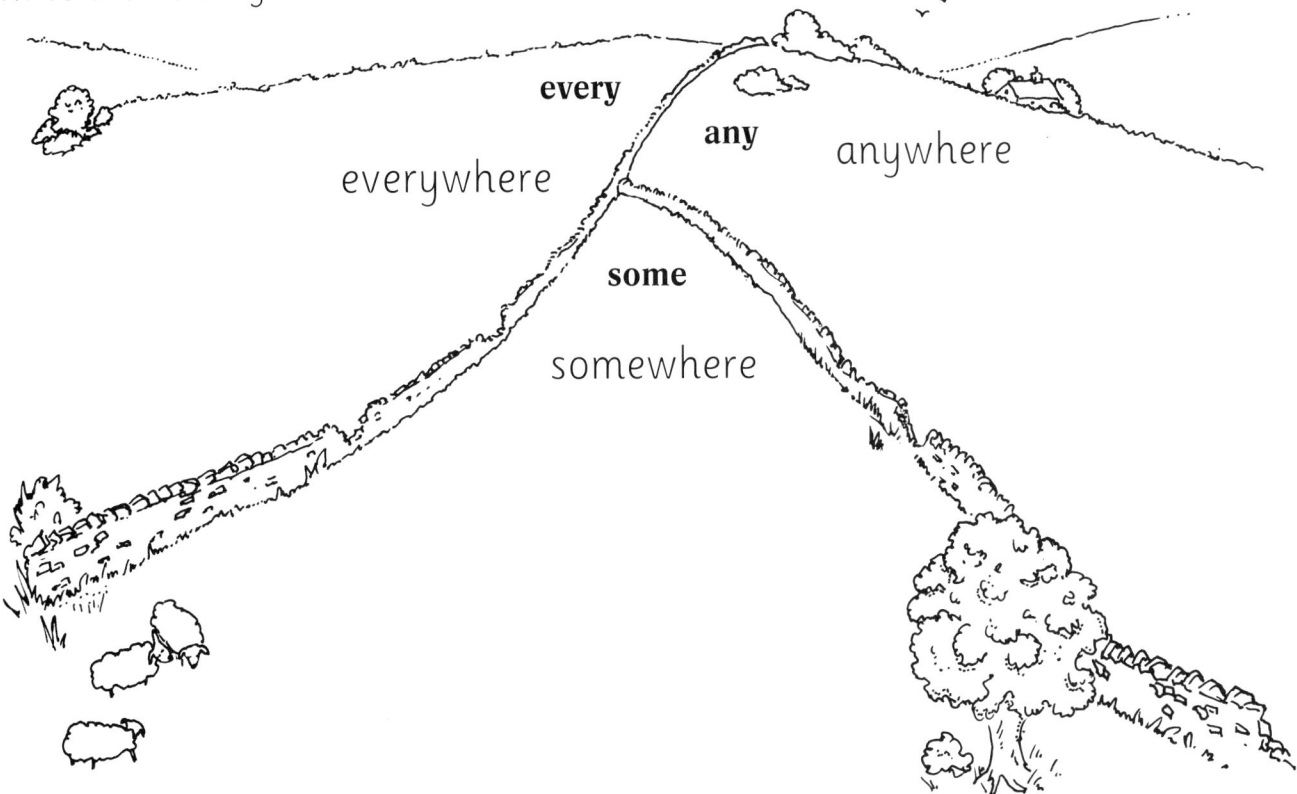

every
everywhere

any
anywhere

some
somewhere

© Cambridge University Press 1997   Original illustrations by Peter Kavanagh

31 Compound words (2) – nouns

Main learning objective

For children to learn to recognise compound words (the focus here is on nouns). Looking at the whole pattern of a word can help them to recognise two familiar words within a compound form.

> **Supporting text**
> *Ben's Amazing Birthday*
> Richard Brown
> Picture and text from page 21

Teaching activities

- Re-read a book to or with the children, listing all the compound words (i.e. those which comprise two base words which can stand alone, such as *birthday*, *bushfires*, *fire-engine*). Most of the words on the worksheet activity come from *Ben's Amazing Birthday*, so you may prefer to choose a different book.
- Ask the children to spot the words within the words in the list. Demonstrate some of the strategies that they should use to spot where word boundaries are likely to fall. Obviously a hyphen helps (e.g. *fire-engine*)! But in its absence, other thought processes may be useful. If they are looking at the word *birthday*, for example, the following should help:
   thd cannot be found as a consonant cluster in one word;
   hd is not a possible word beginning or ending;
   ir is a fixed letter pattern.
   Therefore the first word must be *b–ir–th*.
   Once you have demonstrated this with one word, ask some of the children to explain strategies for looking at other words on the list.

The worksheet

- As the children complete the second part of the worksheet (i.e. underlining the stressed syllables), draw their attention to the fact that the first word in the compound has the main stress (and that it keeps its normal stress if it has two syllables, e.g. j<u>e</u>llyfish). If the second word has two syllables, one of them will be slightly more stressed than the other (e.g. FIRE <u>engine</u>) but the main stress will always be on the first word.
- The words on the worksheet are: *birthday, bushfire, midnight, bedroom, hillside, jellyfish, grandparents, rock-pool, fire-engine.*

Reinforcement and extension

- The children could use books they are familiar with to hunt for compound words with or without hyphens.
- Explain that sometimes a hyphen is used at the extreme right of a line of print to indicate that a word continues on the next line. Ask them to hunt for examples of words hyphenated for this reason (but note that **Cambridge Reading** books do not hyphenate words for this reason at this level).

31

Fire-engine, jellyfish, birthday

Name _____ Date _____

Then I heard sirens. I ran to the **roadside**. Two **fire-engines** rushed past me, up the hill.

The words roadside and fire-engines are made of two words joined together. Make new words by joining together one word from each of these jellyfish. You can only use each word once!

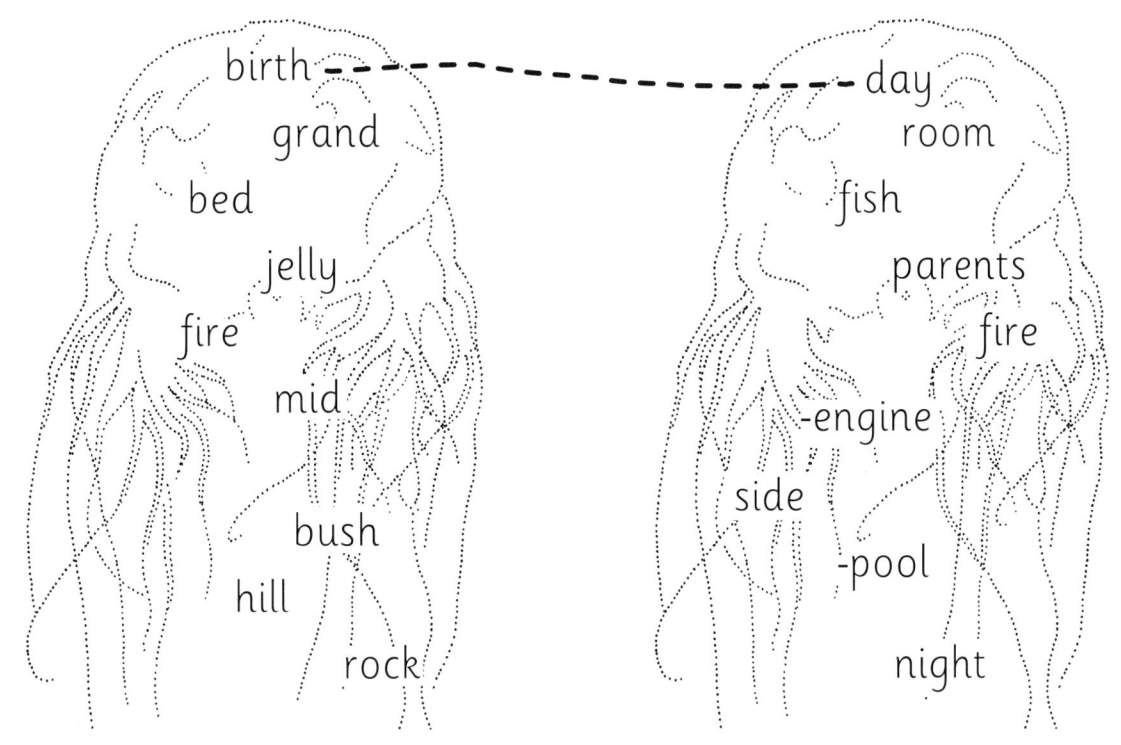

birth — — — day
grand   room
bed   fish
jelly   parents
fire   fire
mid   -engine
           side
bush   -pool
hill
rock   night

Write the new words you made here. Underline the stressed syllable.

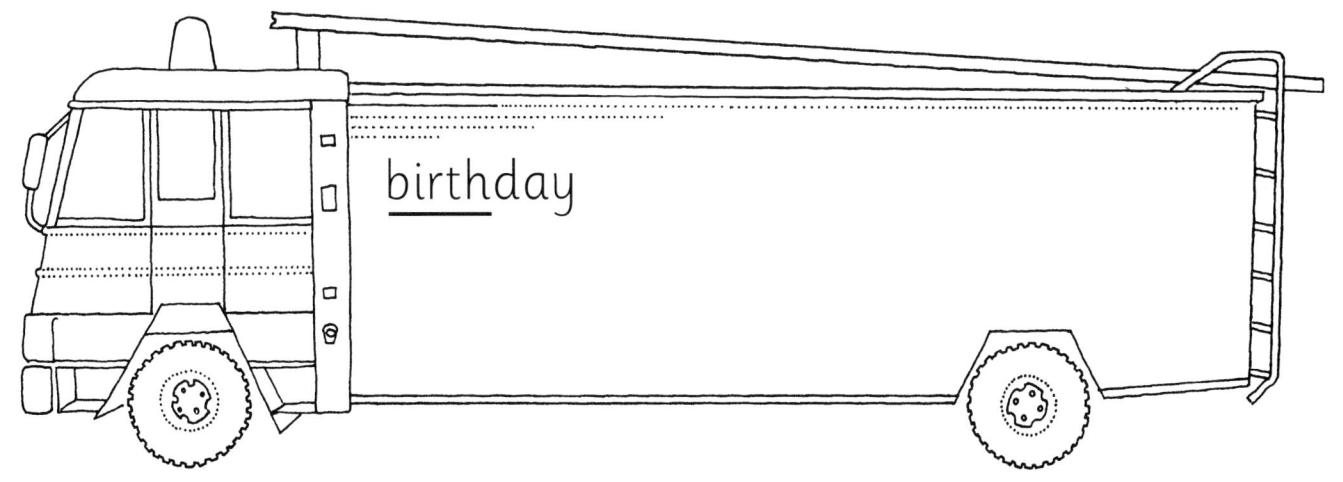

<u>birth</u>day

32 Contractions

Main learning objective

For children to recognise written contracted forms (e.g. *I'll*, *she'd*, *we're*) and to know what base forms they are constructed from.

> **Supporting text**
> *Rabbit's Tail*
> Duncan Williamson and Linda Williamson
> Picture and text from page 3

Teaching activities

- Write a number of contracted forms on the board, ensuring that you have at least one of each of the following types:
    + have (*I've, you've, we've, they've, would've, should've, might've*)
    + had/would (*I'd, you'd, he'd, she'd, we'd, they'd*)
    + will/shall (*I'll, you'll, she'll, he'll, it'll, we'll, they'll*)
    + is/has (*she's, he's, it's, what's, there's, who's*)
    + is (*here's, where's*)
    + am (*I'm*)
    + are (*you're, we're*)
    + us (*let's*)
    + not (*isn't, aren't, can't, couldn't, don't, doesn't, didn't, hasn't, wasn't, wouldn't, won't*)

- Tell the children that the apostrophe represents the missing bit of word. Demonstrate with a few words by writing the full form, then rubbing out the missing letters and substituting an apostrophe.

- Ask different children to suggest what the full form of each of the contractions in your list might be. Write out the full forms so that the children can see how they relate to the contractions.

- Point out to the children that the contracted forms for *had* and *would*, and for *is* and *has*, are the same. They will be able to tell which is correct by seeing which makes good sense in the context of the sentence.

- Draw the children's attention to *won't*, which is the irregular contracted form of *will not*. Then ask them to tell you the full form of *don't*.

- The children should work in groups to compile their own lists of contractions that they use. Point out that they can use proper names (e.g. *Jim's got one*). The groups could swap lists, and another group could write out the full forms of each of the contractions. (Warn them to be careful of *would've*, which is not a contraction of *would of*!)

The worksheet

- Some children may find it helpful, when they come to do the worksheet, if you amend the sheet so that either all the contracted or all the non-contracted forms are filled in.

Reinforcement and extension

- Look at a variety of different books with the children, including information books, searching for contracted forms. Can the children make any observations about when they usually occur? Draw their attention to speech marks, pointing out that a lot of contracted forms occur in speech.

- Select and copy a few pages from a book which

(continued over page)

I'm, we'll, isn't

32

Name _____   Date _____

Hedgehog said, "What shall we do? **He's** bigger than us." Then she said, "**I've** got an idea. **Let's** go and see our friend Fox. **He's** very clever."

Fill in the spaces in these fish. Write down the two full words or the shortened form.

I have	I've
you have	
	we've
they have	

I'll	I will
you'll	
	he will
they'll	

I would	I'd
you would	
	she'd
we would	

I'm	
you're	
	he is
	we are

Fill in the spaces on the fox.

cannot	
	didn't
would not	

could not	
	won't
did not	

© Cambridge University Press 1997   Original illustrations by David Parkins

(*continued from previous page*)

contain a good deal of conversation (try to avoid examples of possessive forms, e.g. *Kate's book*). Give one page to each pair of children and ask them to write out in full each of the contracted forms that they find.

- Ask them to read aloud from both versions, with and without the contracted forms. Discuss with them why the author might have chosen to use contracted forms.
- Point out other common contractions to the children (e.g. *Mr, Mrs* and *Dr*) and discuss why they might be used.
- Once children are secure in their knowledge of contracted forms, you could introduce them to possessive forms (e.g. *Kate's book, Richard's house*). Write two sentences (e.g. *Sima's hair is green* and *Sima's very hungry*). Discuss with the children how they would distinguish the contracted form from the possessive form. Then ask the children to work in pairs to look for examples of each in a familiar book. They should make a list of contracted forms and a list of possessive forms, writing out the sentence each time.

It is worth pointing out to the children that no possessive pronoun should contain an apostrophe (i.e. *mine, yours, his, hers, its, ours, theirs*).